Prejudice Should Grieve Your Heart

THE UNCTION TO INTERCEDE

LYDIA E'ELYON

Published by JCGC Publishers
All rights reserved ©2021

ISBN : 9798375936932
First published : 2023

You are not allowed to duplicate; alter; translate, reproduce or distribute this book for sale or in any manner whatsoever without written permission from the author. Only brief quotations in critical reviews may be allowed.

Unless otherwise cited; Scripture quotations are from the NEW KING JAMES VERSION of the Bible. Copyright © 1979, 1980, 1982, Thomas Nelson, Publishers.

Book cover design by : Allos Parakletos
Email : JCGCpublic@outlook.com

Copyright © 2023 by Lydia E'Elyon
All rights reserved.

TABLE OF CONTENTS

PREFACE	5
1. MY VISIT TO THE SUPREME COURT IN HEAVEN	7
2. IMPARTIALITY	13
3. INTERCEDING FOR JUSTICEE	24
4. NO LAW NO JUSTICE	38
5. THE STANDARD FOR JUSTICE IS LOVE	54
6. TRAITS OF JUSTICE	67
7. JUDGES (DELIVERERS)	82
8. JUDGMENT AND DECLARATION	108
9. PREJUDICE	138
10. JUDICIAL PREJUDICE	151
11. THE INTERCEDER	165
12. THE UNCTION TO INTERCEDE	184
13. THE ANGEL OF JUSTICE	207
14. COOPERATE WITH THE SPIRIT OF JUSTICE	224
SCRIPTURE REFERENCE	239
AUTHOR DIRECTORY	252

Prejudice Should Grieve Your Heart

THE UNCTION TO INTERCEDE

PREFACE

This extra ordinary revelatory book is a capacitor of Biblical insights intended to reveal the dynamics of how the LORD God administers justice to the oppressed and prejudiced. It is through the viewpoint of this Supreme Law of the LORD that we trace the missing puzzle in justice that brings forth lawlessness, oppression and prejudice.

Through this book, you will learn about how the Law of God is a driver of justice and the guide of how justice should function: both in the contemporary magistrate courts, and in the society as part of the lifestyle of the people. Prejudice hurts, it is unwanted!

The book also gives a clear insight about the LORD God overtakes partial justice and assign the Angel of Justice to make judgments to prove that, no one is above the law. A discerning priest in the

Bible said: "If one-man sin against another, the judge shall judge him: but if a man sin against the LORD, who shall intercede for him?" (1 Samuel 2:25).

CHAPTER 1

MY VISIT TO THE SUPREME COURT IN HEAVEN

I was in the realm of the Spirit, and caught up inside the Court room. Inside the court, I was shown a chamber that was introduced to me as the Royal box and a judgment seat. I saw no one there, then I took the exit door. As I stood outside, I saw a bright white curtain with gold and blue trimmings decorated with royal blue tassels. The curtain was let down like a descending cloud from heaven above, and it covered the Court.

"Hmmm! For how long will the Judge be away?" I thought to myself.

The Angel of the LORD spoke to me and explained about this Court. He said that, this is the Court in heaven where the Lord Jesus grants justice to those who are oppressed in the world. The Angel of the LORD told me that, the LORD conducts hearings and judgments on specific times and days of the week. That reminded me of His word when He said: "I can of mine own self do nothing: as I hear, I judge: and My judgment is just; because I seek not mine own will, but the will of the Father who has sent Me" (John 5:30).

MULTITUDES CRY FOR JUSTICE BEFORE THE LORD

On the 5th year, I was lifted again into the realm of the Spirit and I stood in heaven inside the

Courtroom where I saw a commotion of spirits of people pushing to come in and present their cases to the LORD seated on the judgment sea I looked in great amazement and thought to my heart, "Surely these must be the victims of injustices and the raw tooth of prejudice in the world." It was a man of God name John, he saw a similar vision and the Angel of the LORD explained to him about the people that he saw: "These are they which came out of great tribulation, and have washed their robes, and made them white in the blood of the Lamb" (Revelation 7:14-15).

EVIDENCE IN VIDEO RECORDS

It seems clear that the LORD attends to every matter that pertains to the suffering of all people on earth, as long as they give Him that attention, as His word says; "Asked and it shall be given you." **"He has regarded the prayer of the destitute and has not despised their appeal"** (Psalm 102:17).

Paul the Apostle whilst teaching about righteousness also foretold the Corinthian Church about the judgment seat in Heaven, and he said, **"For we must all appear before the judgment seat of Christ;** that every one may receive the things done in his body, according to that he has done, whether it be good or bad" (2 Corinthians 5:10).

Then, I saw the Lord Jesus sitting in the Royal Box and hearing different cases and I recall the words of the Apostle who said:

"Through this Jesus is preached unto you the forgiveness of sins: And by Him all that believe are justified from all things, from

which you could not be justified by the Law of Moses" (Acts 13:38-39).

Synonym to this same truth, one may say that, if you believe in this same Lord Jesus, you will be justified from all things from which you could not be justified, even by the hash laws of the nations. What I noticed was that, there was pitched before the Lord as very huge screen which my spirit perceived to be a video record of crimes and offences of those whose cases were presented in the hearings. Those video records are presented as testimonies against the offenders.

"…they are the eyes of the LORD, which run to and fro through the whole earth" (Zechariah 4:10). There is no secret or anything hidden which cannot be revealed before the LORD, and His judgments are true.

"Surely there is a reward for the righteous; surely there is a God who judges on earth!" (Psalm 58:11).

The Lord Jesus then turned to me, and allowed me to present my petition. He did not delay to involve His Spirit (Angel) to look into these matters, and His verdicts will be fair. Then I returned from the realm of the spirit feeling much justified.

"The LORD loves righteousness and justice; the earth is full of His unfailing love" (Psalm 33:5).

CHAPTER 2

IMPARTIALITY

The LORD God has declared that the foundations of His throne are righteousness and justice (Psalm 89:14). In other words, He is *Jehovah Elohim Mishpat*, the God of Justice. God is very close to the broken hearted, and as a righteous judge He vindicates everyone fairly. Only God is truly, fully, and meaningfully just.

The LORD understands that, there are always cases which may be difficult to be judged or acquitted by a human judge due to their conditions which may not be outlined in the Law of that State. This may include some cases of animosity which may not even be believable, or sound reasonable to the judge; and yet shows emotionally grief to the offended, but with no or limited evidence. The LORD sees what happens in darkness where no one else was there to give evidence, apart from the offended and the offender.

"Therefore judge nothing before the time, until the Lord come, who both will bring to light the hidden things of darkness, and will make manifest the counsels of the hearts" (1 Corinthians 4:5).

Therefore, whenever all the justice systems of the world have failed to give you justice, and you see your case handled with prejudice; it is very important not to give up your life to death. Turn around, be strong and humbly present your appeal to the LORD God your creator and Father.

IMPARTIALITY IS A CRY OF EVERY HEART

All over the world, most hearts of the oppressed palpitates with grief every day that they enter the court for a hearing. Their eyes look with hope into the eyes of the judge, and hope for justice against their adversaries, and they can no longer wait for the Day of Judgment.

The desperation of the oppressed to receive deliverance shows that justice abides in the spirit of man, and the statutes of the LORD says that **"He will not look with contempt a broken and humbled heart"** (Psalms 51:17). Which means that, as the oppressed looks to the judge for justice, the LORD God watches the proceedings and entrusts fair justice in the heart of the judge.

This may take us to the concurrent words of King Jehoshaphat where he admonished the judges that he had appointed in Israel:

"Consider what you are doing, for you do not judge for man but for the LORD who is with you when you render judgment."

"Now then let the fear of the LORD be upon you; **be very careful what you do, for the LORD our God will have no part in unrighteousness or partiality or the taking of a bribe"** (2 Chronicles 19:6-7).

Therefore, as a good lord standing in the name of the LORD God, the judge is expected to function as an impartial referee, and ensure correct procedure, while the prosecution and the defense present their case to a jury. A judge must NOT be the judge in a case that he or she has a negative or positive interest. "…why do you regard your brother with contempt? For we will all stand before the judgment seat of God" (Romans 14:10).

Impartiality is a very important for rule of law, therefore a judge is not insusceptible to judgment for his or her acts of prejudice. A judge is expected to conduct a trial impartially and, typically, in an open court as the LORD said:

"I have not spoken in secret, in a dark place of the earth" (Isaiah 45:19) [Isaiah 48:16].

IMPARTIALITY ASSURES JUSTICE

Where the Supreme Law of Love rules in the heart of a judge, every individual involved in a matter that the judge is presiding on will all be treated as the image of God, with respect, dignity, and equality without any actual or apparent partiality. It must also remain a fundamental code of the administration of justice that, those who appear before the courts are treated fairly, and that judges act fairly and impartially throughout the trial process.

For in the first place, when God created mankind, He did it without prejudice, but He said to His superior Spirit; **"Let us make man in our image, after our likeness"** (Genesis 1:26). Then, once a judge is in this attitude, he or she will judge every matter with integrity without prejudice.

He or she will rule out and unleash a fair judgment. "If you really fulfill the royal law (Love) according to the Scripture, **"You shall love your neighbor as yourself,"** you are doing well. But if you show partiality, you are committing sin and are convicted by the law as transgressors" (James 2:8-9). God views this kind of prejudice, partiality, and discrimination as sin.

DO YOU PULL A FELLOW BELIEVER TO THE COURT?

A person who has not yet believed in the Lord Jesus, who happens to have an issue with a Christian and feels that she or he needs justice, this person may freely take the issue to the court, and the Christian must not resist to go to face the judge in the open court concerning the matter. But, people who are both Christians are not supposed to deliver one another in public courts, because there is the Spirit of Justice in the house of God.

"My house shall be called the house of prayer" (Matthew 21:13).

As it was dedicated in the book of 1st Kings 8:31-32: "If a man sins against his neighbor and is made to take an oath, and he comes and takes an oath before Your altar in this house, then hear in heaven and judge, condemning the wicked by bringing his way on his own head, and justifying the righteous by giving him according to his righteousness."

Dragging a fellow Christian to a public court over petite issues like divorce, leadership conflicts, business partnership disagreements, charities and offerings issues is a sign that you have broken the Law of Love.

"Confess your faults one to another, and pray one for another" (James 5:16).

Unless the fellow has conformed back to the world, and has broken the law in such acts like: assassination, adultery, robbery, theft, ritual murder, hijacking, bribery, fraud and money laundering, sodomy, rape, hiring henchmen, piracy, sedition, abducting, bullying, abusing, lies, abortion, witchcraft, sorcery, terrorism, and more other crimes. Committing such things rules out this one *is not or is no longer* a Christian, and must indeed be cast out of the house of prayer, because a true Christians is not supposed to do such things, and neither is it possible to do them if truly born of the Holy Spirit and still in Him.

"Therefore put away from among yourselves that wicked person" (1 Corinthians 5:13).

Christians have the Law of the LORD within their hearts. It judges them always, and whenever they have a disagreement with one another over a trifle or issues, the LORD expects them to assemble before Him in His house and pray over that issue, and the Spirit of the LORD will judge and give the ruling. Devout Christians know this, and they have proven it through much evidence in their personal lives that it works, and thus Christians live in peace and love amongst themselves and supposed to love every other person not withstanding their religion or anything.

"Do you not know that the saints will judge the world? If the world is judged by you, are you not competent to constitute the smallest law courts? **Do you not know that we will judge angels? How much more matters of this life?**

So if you have law courts dealing with matters of this life, do you appoint them as judges who are of no account in the church? Is it possible that no one among you is wise enough to judge matters between believers?

Instead, one believer goes to court against another. And this happens in front of unbelievers! When you take another believer to court, you have lost the battle already. Why not be treated wrongly? Why not be cheated? Instead, you yourselves cheat and do wrong. And you do it to your brothers and sisters. Don't you know that people who do wrong will not receive God's kingdom? Don't be fooled" (1 Corinthians 6:2-11).

CHAPTER 3

INTERCEDING FOR JUSTICE

Another local church committed a grave sin against the LORD God. It was like the act of Aaron who presented a golden calf to the people saying: "These are your gods, O Israel, which delivered you out of the land of Egypt" (Exodus 32:4). My very close friend troubled me about not joining the group of church intercessors. She was a very strong intercessor, and under the department of intercessors. She always felt like I am another missing link in their interceding group. They used to gather together at church from 6:30 A.M and take turns praying throughout the service. I preferred to remain in my prayer closet, and have fellowship with the LORD, then go to church when the main service was about to start. But my friend troubled me until one day I heard the Holy Spirit say to me; **"Today, you must go, and intercede with them."**

Therefore, I went there boldly and excited, because I had a go ahead from the LORD. I found the team praying in the Spirit, and bubbling in great tongues. Already there were thousands of people standing outside the church gates and waiting for the doors to open. Upon seeing the multitude as they kept coming and standing there like sheep; I was moved with compassion to intercede for them that all may be free, and be touched by the LORD. I engaged in prayer, and propitiated the LORD for the outbreak of spontaneous healings and deliverance.

In about five minutes whilst I was still interceding, and asking the LORD to cause the Devil to remove his dirty hand prints from the lives of the people of God. I heard the voice of the LORD speak in my hearing clearly, and He questioned me: "Is it to Me that these multitudes have come?" That question froze my whole body. I knelt down, and became motionless. "Oh' my God, my God!" I remained with an unanswered question in my heart.

"If it is not for the LORD, then to who have they come?" My friend noticed that something perplexing was going on in my spirit. She came to me and asked, **"Is everything alright?"** My heart was already grieved. But I was strengthened, and I told her what the LORD spoke in my hearing. She became distraught in her spirit, but we did not tell anyone else about it. I prayed for mercy, and forgiveness on behalf of the multitude who had sinned –coming to worship something else in His church rather than God.

I prayed for repentance to come to their hearts; and I left that intercession area, and never returned to pray with the interceders ever again. On the following day the overseer of the church, a great prophet of God, stood before the congregation after preaching that evening. And he said;

"You people have caused me trouble with God. I have seen two angels of the LORD turn their backs on me, and they left me." "Then I asked the LORD, why are the angels leaving me? "And God told me that,

"It is because the people are now worshiping you, and they have stopped worshiping Me." **"Now therefore tell your people to desist from worshiping you."**

The whole church, and the man of God

bowed down, and repented from the great sin of idolatry. And the angels were restored at that time.

INTERCEDING FOR ONE WHO SINNED AGAINST THE LORD GOD

An intercessor prophet has power to entreat God to relent from heavy judgment against His people who sinned. However, there are cases which are very difficult for judges, because the offender has offended God.

Some of those cases may be solved by asking God a way forward to the matter, and as some may not be resolved unless He Himself passes the judgment.

There is a period of serving punishment from God for every offender who offends God;

this period is called the *consummation of sin*. Most people who get these punishments are people of high level authority like kings, rulers, leaders, and rebels. King David once experienced such punishment after his sin of taking the census of his subjects: Study the cases below.

"David felt ashamed after he had counted the people. He said to the LORD, "I have sinned greatly by what I have done. LORD, I beg you to forgive me, your servant, because I have been very foolish." When David got up in the morning, the LORD spoke his word to Gad, who was a prophet and David's seer. The LORD told Gad, **"Go and tell David, 'this is what the LORD says: I offer you three choices. Choose one of them and I will do it to you.'"**

So Gad went to David and said to him, "Should three years of hunger come to you and your land? Or should your enemies chase you for three months? Or should there be three days of disease in your land? Think about it. Then decide which of these things I should tell the LORD who sent me."

David said to Gad, "I am in great trouble. Let the LORD punish us, because the LORD is very merciful. Don't let my punishment come from human beings!" So the LORD sent a terrible disease on Israel.

It began in the morning and continued until the chosen time to stop. From Dan to Beersheba seventy thousand people died. When the angel raised his arm toward Jerusalem to destroy it, the LORD felt very sorry about the terrible things that had happened. **He said to the angel who was destroying the people, "That is enough! Put down your arm!"**

The Angel of the LORD was then by the threshing floor of Araunah the Jebusite. When David saw the angel that killed the people, he said to the LORD, "I am the one who sinned and did wrong. These people only followed me like sheep. They did nothing wrong. Please punish me and my family" (1 Samuel 24:10-17).

King Nebuchadnezzar was to live like a wild beast and eat grass and chew a cad for a period of years until he came the period of his judgment lapsed.

Often times Moses was the only prophet who was able to tell God to repent from His anger against His people who offended Him. But after he had offended God no judge could intercede for him.

The Bible records another difficult case which could not be resolved between King Saul and the LORD. As a result, Samuel could not receive a favorable answer for King Saul from the LORD after interceding for him.

Although Saul was a judge himself, he

lost his case against the LORD of lords. That meant the loss of his kingdom permanently as judgment from the LORD. As priest Eli admonished his wicked sons:

"If one-man sin against another, the judge shall judge him: but if a man sin against the LORD, who shall intercede for him?" (1 Samuel 2:25).

And so, the LORD spoke to Samuel concerning interceding for Saul and He said; **"How long will you cry for Saul seeing I have rejected him"** (1 Samuel 16:1). And that is how Saul's case was closed.

A CASE OF A COMMUNITY THAT SINNED AGAINST THE LORD

Study this case and learn how the kings who followed the move of the Spirit of God bringing a revival influenced the governing of the people with regards to obeying the law of God, and His statutes.

Learn the importance of harmony in a nation through obeying judges and applying God's laws against the discord, and curses that was upon a people who broke the law of God:

Case: *Intermarriage with pagans.*

Offender: *About 200 men of Jerusalem (listed in Ezra 10:18-44).*

Complainant: *the LORD God*
Conditions: *Whoever will not come to the court*

within three days according to the instruction will have his property confiscated (Ezra 10:8).

Charge: the men married pagan women, and trespassed God's commandment according to His Law:

"You shall not make any covenant with them, no show mercy to them." Nor shall you make marriages with them.

You shall not give your daughter to their son, no take their daughter for your son. For they will turn your sons from following Me, to serve other gods; so the anger of the LORD will be aroused against you and destroy you suddenly" (Deuteronomy 7:2-4).

1st Confession /Testimony –To God: *Ezra lays charge against the men who married pagan women– Standing for God* (Ezra 10:1)

2nd Confession/ Testimony –To the

Judge: *"Shechaniah son of Jehiel "We have trespassed against our God, and have taken pagan wives from the peoples of the land" (Ezra 10:2).*

Representatives: *(Elders)"Let our leaders represent the whole assembly and let all those in our cities who have married foreign wives come at appointed times, together with the elders and judges of each city, until the fierce anger of our God on account of this matter is turned away from us" (Ezra 10:14).*

Judge: *New Judges* appointed by Ezra according to a decree authorizing him by King Artaxerxes: *"You, Ezra, according to the wisdom of your God which is in your hand, appoint magistrates and judges that they may judge all the people who are in the province beyond the River, even all those who know the laws of your God; and you may teach anyone who is ignorant of them" (Ezra 7:25-26).*

Profile of Ezra: <u>Governor</u> *of Jerusalem, given a* decree by King Darius to facilitate the building of the house of God in Jerusalem, financed by taxes from the king's treasury (Ezra 6:1-23).

A <u>Skilled scribe</u> in the Law of Moses, which the LORD God of Israel had given, and had the hand of the LORD God upon him (Ezra 7:6) (Ezra 7:10) (Ezra 7:11).

He was a full time <u>intercessor (priest of God)</u> and is seen praying to God and asking help from Him for every matter (Ezra 8:21-28).

All that Ezra did was in God's agenda according to the word of the LORD given through prophet Jeremiah: "Now in the first year of Cyrus king of Persia--in order to fulfill the word of the LORD by the mouth of Jeremiah.
The LORD stirred up the spirit of Cyrus king of Persia, so that he sent a proclamation throughout his kingdom, and also put it in writing, saying, "Thus says

Cyrus king of Persia, 'The LORD, the God of heaven, has given me all the kingdoms of the earth, and He has appointed me to build Him a house in Jerusalem, which is in Judah.

Whoever there is among you of all His people, may the LORD his God be with him, and let him go up!'" (2 Chronicles 36:22-23). (Ezra 1:1-4).

Duration of Hearing the Case: *5 months (From the 12th of the 9th Month of the year —Ezra 10:9) "By the first day of the first month they had finished questioning all the men who had taken pagan wives" (Ezra 10:17).*
Outcome: *Men who married pagan women all guilty.*
Judgment/ Verdict: *Separate from pagan wives and let them go with their children.*
Penalties: *Guilty charged Trespass offering —a ram of the flock each (Ezra 10:19).* Case was ended with mercy, as no man was condemned to death.

CHAPTER 4

NO LAW
NO JUSTICE

The LORD God has founded His principles of justice upon His Law and statutes which He gave to His people. As you look up to Him for justice or deliverance, it is important to know that He does nothing outside what He has commanded (the Law). "For the LORD is our judge, The LORD is our lawgiver, The LORD is our king; He will save us" (Isaiah 33:22).

Therefore, it is very important to know the Supreme Law of the LORD, so that the adversary and oppressor does not take advantage to humiliate you, nor you should not do the opposite because you will be judged by the same Law.

THE BACKGROUND OF THE SUPREME LAW OF GOD

Imagine yourself in a country or an institution where there is no law or a person who live without principles? Without the Law there is no good governance or order of doing things. A kingdom cannot run smoothly without a governing body of laws.

Under every regime, a moral and civil law is put in place to build, and give people good values and norms through the righteous deeds performed through obeying it; and that's how a distinct family or nation is formed. Are you spiritual? Remember that the Lord Jesus said that, He did not come to abolish the law and the prophets but to justify it, (Matthew 5:17-18).

The Law of God has not conceded, but has been justified. Meaning that, its statutes that it commanded the former generation was reviewed and observed by the present generation. The prophets were the declarers of the law and judgments of the LORD God. Through the promise given to father Abraham, God's plan was to use the nation Israel as a model to demonstrate to the world how a nation can develop by obeying the law.

Also, how the law watches against prejudice, crime and oppression to establish justice within a nation in order to maintain peace and stability something which was not common in the world. The plan of the LORD God about Abraham was for his children to walk according His law. This is contrary to the standards of the lawless nations which practised perversion.

This plan was revealed by the Angel of

Justice on His way to investigate the land of Gomorrah and Sodom, where lawlessness was reported to have escalated the full measure of sin. This is what the LORD said:

"For I know him, that he will command his children and his household after him, and they shall keep the way of the LORD, **to do justice and judgment; that the LORD may bring upon Abraham that which he has spoken of him**" (Genesis 18:19).

Through Christ Jesus, the validation of this law of God brought forth a universal Supreme Law designed to paranormally govern every individual on earth. For which, breaking that Universal Supreme Law of God is the same as breaking the rest of the common and moral laws of the people of the land.

"For all the law is fulfilled in one word, even

in this; Thou shalt <u>love</u> your neighbour as thyself" (Galatian 5:14).

After the former Law of God was justified by the Lord Jesus, He handed over the New Supreme Law that is relevant to the present time to form **"a chosen generation, a royal priesthood, an holy nation, a peculiar people of God's own possession"** (1 Peter 2:9).

This nation under the new Law is taken out of darkness where individuals practiced all various manners of lawlessness. By the new Law inscribed into their hearts, now the citizens walk into His marvellous light, and show forth the praise of Him.

According to the book of Psalms, one learns that the application of the law in one's life yields prosperity. Which means, the law is good for the wellbeing of a person and his or her works.

"Blessed is the man that walks not in the counsel of the ungodly, nor stands in the way of sinners, nor sits in the seat of the scornful. But his delight is in the law of the LORD; and in his law doth he meditate day and night. And he shall be like a tree planted by the rivers of water, that brings forth his fruit in his season; his leaf also shall not wither; and whatsoever he does shall prosper" (Psalm 1: 1-4).

In the time past, these who were judged by the law were wicked and oppressors, but now, they are a people of God. Through the forgiveness of sin, they have obtained mercy and are justified by the New Supreme Law (Love). This new law does not require any sacrifice of animal blood to cleanse a person from iniquity, and transgressions.

MOSES'S PREDICTED THE NEW LAW

Moses the writer of the first Law of God said that, "The LORD your God will raise up for you a Prophet…like unto me; unto him you shall listen" (Deuteronomy 18:15). Indeed upon hearing this, one would imagine another prophet who would decode from God, and give another Law as a way of bringing lawless lives to order.

The question would be, the Law of Moses was very difficult for the people, although the fear of it chastened their behaviour so that they may live upright. However, would the new law give an ease of access? Christ Jesus came as that prophesied and expected prophet. He brought the new Law which is simple and has keys of ease of access to a justified joyful life and a key of justice.

Jesus introduced the Law of God as a very

important mind boggling matter of the heart (LOVE).

This is unlike the former Law which focused on the outward flesh. He Himself practised the same New Law (Love) in giving justice to the oppressed. Like many legislators today, the Pharisees did not practice the rule of law, but distorted the purpose of the law of God until it transformed into a burden that could no longer release the oppressed. Instead, it weighed heavier upon their oppression to the point that, they began to cry for the coming of the promised Messiah (Deliverer).

The experts of the Law of Moses extremely used the old Law to oppress the people further by making the law as an emphasis that only appeal to the flesh, but neglected the issues of the evil detects of a heart which leads to lawlessness and injustices.

Therefore, the former Law was imposed as a Law that was without mercy, for it could not save or deliver the captives and oppressed in all spheres of life. Failure to apply it as the original good Law of God, motivated the Jewish legal team to put another handwriting over the writing of the Angel of Justice that wrote the Law with Moses.

The handwriting of the Pharisees forged many ordinances which were written against the people. Thus, the Law became like a physical practice, or custom that could be associated to a smart or expensive garment that the people could wear as long as they were in the public eye only; instead of a spiritual emblem of changing attitude towards injustice against self and others.

Jesus observed these issues of the distortion of the Law of God (Law of Moses) and addressed the Lawyers and the Pharisees who were radical extremist of the distorted practise of the Law of God given through Moses:

"Woe to you experts in law! You weigh men down with burdens hard to carry, but you yourselves do not lift one finger to remove them" (Luke 11:46).

The New Testament Bible has more records of officials who were legal legislators known as lawyers. The biblical lawyers were bias in the sense that, although they had studied the Law in scriptures and were well knowledgeable about the LORD's principles of justice, but they disregarded and did not apply the Law in their own personal lives. That wrongly motivated people to act with partiality against one another until a majority of people in Israel lived as hypocrites.

Without the law in their hearts, they began to easily adopt forbidden evil practices of other neighboring countries, and brought judgment upon themselves, which made their lives even more difficult.

There arose foundational hypocritical heroes of the law who knew the Law, but practicing it not at heart. Jesus rebuked the Pharisees and the lawyers for their hypocrisy saying: **"…you have omitted the weightier matters of the law, judgment, mercy, and faith:** these ought ye to have done, and not to leave the other undone" (Matthew 23:23).

THE NEW LAW

"Blotting out **the handwriting of ordinances that was against us,** which was contrary to us, and took it out of the way, nailing it to his cross" (Colossian 2:14).

The New Supreme Law of God is very active today. It governs the kingdom of God in heaven and here on earth, and produces a righteous transformation in human hearts. This transformation influences justice, and harmony in the application of any country's laws that is designed to govern the people in uprightness for their own good, and prosperity.

The Lord Jesus was often times accused of breaking the Law of God which was commanded through Moses the prophet. In the trial that led to His death sentence, the Lord Jesus was charged with treason. This is the highest crime of rebelling the laws of the state. Below is part of their testimony at the Roman court according to the Book of Nicodemus:

Pilate asked: "And what things are they that he does, and would destroy the law?"

The Jews alleged: "We have a law that we should not heal any man on the Sabbath: but this man of his evil deeds hath healed the lame and the bent, the withered and the blind and the paralytic, the dumb and them that were possessed, on the Sabbath day!"

Pilate asked them: "By what evil deeds?"
They say unto him: "He is a sorcerer, and by Beelzebub the prince of the devils he casts out devils, and they are all subject unto him."

By healing the sick, Jesus was not breaking the Law, but fulfilling or justifying the law in the area where it was undermined. The amendment of an existing law, is for the good of the people, so that the portion of the law which could not be applied with relevance may be reviewed and adjusted.

That is what the Lord Jesus was doing.

Until the new law is found and effected, the old law remains active.

After the Messiah took His seat to judge and liberate the people from the oppressive Law, He made an amendment that was long waited and He gave the new Law.

"For the priesthood being changed, there is made of necessity a change also of the law" (Hebrews 7:11-12).

The former Law which had many decrees and regulations which were too hard for people to fulfil was summarised by the Lord Jesus to a one word law: **Love**. The constitution of this Supreme Law of God (Love) comprises of the two Great Commandments:

(i) Love God and have no other gods apart from Him
(ii) Love your fellow citizen (neighbour) as

you love yourself (Love people).

"This is His commandment: that we should believe on the name of His Son Jesus Christ, and love one another, as He gave us commandment. And he that keeps His commandments dwells in Him, and He in him. And hereby we know that He abides in us, by the Spirit which He has given us" (1 John 3:23-24).

As we simplify this constitution, a careful contrast between the two shows that this Supreme Law of God which is termed *Love,* is the LORD God Himself:

"God is love" (1 John 4:16). His nature and His Law therefore is Love.

"Whoever does not love, does not know God, because God is love" (1 John 4:8).

"God so love the world that He gave His only begotten Son, that whosoever believeth in

Him should not perish, but have everlasting life. For God sent not His Son into the world to condemn the world; but that the world through Him might be saved" (John 3:16-17).

CHAPTER 5

THE STANDARD FOR JUSTICE IS LOVE

The foundation of the government of the kingdom of God is firstly, the Law which produces righteousness, justice and equity. It judges the cause of killing, destruction, oppression, sickness, killing, sin, unbelief, and unrighteousness. Therefore, believers overcome the power of sin, and offending others by Love which is the standard for justice.

Through the same standard of justice, to judge another person who has broken the law is an act of injustice, if you are not a judge. For even if you do so, and punish the wrong doer by yourself, you will also be judged by the law for that. Only Law has the right scale of measure of punishment for every evil deed. Even with matters of punishing your own children, according to the Law of God, the right scale for punishing a child is striking by a rod. More than that, it is breaking the law.

"Judge not, that you be not judged" (Matthew 7:1).

"Do not say, I will recompense evil; but wait on the LORD, and He shall save you" (Proverbs 20:22).

Rather let the law take its cause, and a judge who is in authority judge the lawbreaker according to

the just measure. It does not matter how much you have been wronged, but do not judge.
This is a principle that gives the law its power to function, and a foundation to trust in it.

"If you judge the law, you art not a doer of the law, but a judge. There is one lawgiver, who is able to save and to destroy: who art thou that judges another?" (James 4:11-12).

As a believer in Christ Jesus, your sense of justice is imparted to you by the love of God. He is loving, kind, merciful, and He is also righteous, holy, and just.

"The Rock, His work is perfect, for all his ways are justice. A God of faithfulness and without iniquity, just and upright is He" (Deuteronomy 32:4).

Love is the greatest commandment that balances all universal laws as explained here by the Lord Jesus.

"Thou shalt love the Lord thy God with all thy heart, and with all thy soul, and with all thy mind. This is the first and great commandment. And the second is like unto it, *Thou shalt love thy neighbour as thyself.* On these two commandments hang all the law and the prophets" (Matthew 22:37-40).

SETTING THE STANDARD

The commandment or Law of Love is the Standard or Rule of Law of the Kingdom of God on earth, and it enhances harmony and peace when applied to any civil or moral law of a nation.

"A new commandment I give to you, that you love one another: just as I have loved you, you also are to love one another" (John 13:34).

In the judicial law, the standards make it easier to demonstrate that, one has followed best practices. In the face of Love the Son of Justice, there is no partiality or prejudice, but fairness becomes the outcome of righteous judgment.

"Let no debt remain outstanding, except the continuing debt to love one another, for whoever loves others has fulfilled the law" (1 Corinthians 2:9 NIV).

God is just. It is part of His character, which means He is always just. He cannot be unjust, and He defines and sets the standard for justice as you have read. "Righteousness and justice are the foundation of your throne; steadfast love and faithfulness go before you" (Psalm 89:14). The standard is an instrument of deregulation which helps relieve the legislative burden on the legislator.

Thus, legislators can concentrate on overall issues and protection objectives of the law and justice without imposing more regulations or restrictions on anyone who already knows the law.

"To those who are in Christ, there is no law. For the law brings wrath. And where there is no law there is no transgression" (Romans 4:15).

This does not mean that the kingdom of God is lawless, otherwise then, it would embrace acts of lawlessness. But this means that you need not to be monitored; because you have the constitution of the law of the LORD God within your heart.

It is always guiding you through righteousness, and sets the standard for you, so that you may be able to resist the evil force and temptations of lawlessness. If you have love, you would not sin against God, for you love Him, nor sin against fellow man for you love him as yourself. Therefore, the law will not find any fault in you to judge against you, because the Law of love rules in you bearing "love, joy, peace, longsuffering, gentleness, goodness, faith, meekness, temperance (self-control). Against such things there is no judgment.

According to the former Law (Law of Moses), people were physically monitored to check if they have subjected themselves to the law. This was because, that kind of law was only working in their minds as a given statute, but not in their hearts as a divine Law. So they often times fell short and judged for transgressing the law. This applies to every earthly law that is designed to govern people.

People break it, and get arrested, whilst others thrive to hide the evidence of their wickedness. Others bribe corrupt authorities or the judge, meantime the oppressed cry foul to the LORD. All this happens because the basic divine Law of God which is supposed to regulate a person's heart is not yet inscribed in the hearts.

"The heart is deceitful above all things, and desperately wicked: who can know it? **I the LORD searches the heart, I try the reins, even to give every man according to his ways, and according to the fruit of his doings"** (Jeremiah 17:9-10).

Thus, the use of the laws of the people in

the world without love is a preaching without practise, and hypocritical code used to bluff people's eyes. When eyes turn around the law is done, but when eyes are off there are woes of lawlessness.

"For all who have sinned without the Law will also perish without the Law, and all who have sinned under the Law will be judged by the Law; for it is not the hearers of the Law who are just before God, but the doers of the Law will be justified" (Romans 2:12-16).

It is through God's standard then, that there is order and harmony within our beings, and amongst us as members of the body of Christ –the royal priesthood and citizens of Heaven on earth. The Lord Jesus sets the boundaries for that which is unjust, and what is just and act in accordance to the perfect standard of the Law and justice. Deuteronomy 32:4 says,

"The Rock, his work is perfect, for all His ways are justice. A God of faithfulness and without iniquity, just and upright is He."

Any eccentricity to the justice of the LORD is judged *"unfair."* Actions that align with the standard of the LORD are considered *"unprejudiced."* Therefore, The LORD as the God of Justice, does not only set the standard, He does that which is congruence with that standard. In His Infinite Holy self, is the ultimate standard —Love.

"The works of His hands are faithful and just; all His precepts are trustworthy; they are established forever and ever, to be performed with faithfulness and uprightness" (Psalm 111:7-8).

The book of Isaiah tells us that when the enemy comes in like a flood, **the Spirit of the Lord will lift up a standard against him** (Isaiah 59:19).

The lifting up of the standard speaks of the declaration of righteous judgments through Him who judges justly. We know from the testimony of Nicodemus that the Roman high court raised the Roman law's standard at the trial of Jesus Christ, and it was then that the wife of Pilate came in to inform Pilate to have nothing to do with that innocent man (Jesus).

It followed after this incidence that Pilate washed his hands and handed Jesus over to the Jews and told them to judge Him *according to their own Law.* Unfortunately, they had no Jewish Intercessor (Judge) to take up the case, so they had to proceed with the Roman Judge, Pilate.

The elders of the Jews took twelve men strong and able and made them to hold the standards by sixes, and they were set before the judgment-seat of the governor; and Pilate said to the messenger: Take him out of the judgment hall (praetorium) and bring him in again after what manner thou wilt.

And Jesus went out of the judgment hall, He and the messenger. And Pilate called unto him them that before held the image and said unto them: I have sworn by the safety of Caesar that *if the standards bow* not when Jesus entered in, I will cut off your heads.

And the governor commanded Jesus to enter in the second time. And the messenger did after the former manner and besought Jesus much that he would walk upon his kerchief; and he walked upon it and entered in. **And when he had entered, the standards bowed** themselves again and did reverence unto Jesus""

"Now when Pilate also considered how the standards bowed to Jesus, he was afraid, and sought to rise up from the judgement-seat."

And while he yet thought to rise up, his wife sent unto him, saying: Have thou nothing to do with this just man, for I have suffered many things because of him by night" (Gospel by Nicodemus).

CHAPTER 6

TRAITS OF JUSTICE

The Most High LORD is indeed just, His statutes are pure, and in Him there is no propaganda nor prejudice. "He does execute the judgment of the fatherless and widow, and loves the stranger, in giving him food and raiment. Love therefore the stranger" (Deuteronomy 10:17-19).

WHAT IS JUSTICE?

Justice is a devout decree prescribed by the LORD as a lawful right to an individual or people. Justice may be the right thing or action accorded as a means of deliverance to the oppressed. A right of ownership to the defrauded or deprived proprietor. A right of protection from an offender. Using force or fraud to exploit the vulnerable is evil. A release from any kind of rocky burden of oppression that makes livelihood difficult or makes life itself to be bitter.

Here is an example of an appeal for justice:

"At the end of seven years, the woman returned from the land of the Philistines; and she went out to appeal to the king for

her house and for her field" (2 Kings 8:3).

Here is an example of Justice:

"When the king asked the woman, she related it to him. So the king appointed for her a certain officer, saying, Restore all that was hers and all the produce of the field from the day that she left the land even until now" (2 Kings 8:6).

THE PRACTICAL ROOT OF JUSTICE

The world needs order, fairness, and justice. The people in this world lack the ability to judge their evil deeds, because their version of right and wrong is misconstrued.

"Evildoers do not understand what is

right, but those who seek the LORD understand it fully" (Proverbs 28:5).

Justice is rooted in the compassionate love of the LORD, the creator of heaven and the universe. There is nothing in this universe that God created for chaos, because He is in Himself just and is the God of order. That's why when there was darkness in the beginning, He created light to conquer the darkness by day and by night, and He also gave form to the formless earth so that it may exhibit His order.

Where justice is appropriately applied, there is a rule of law. The rule of law is the civil belief that all citizens and foundations within a country, state, or community are accountable to the same constitutional law. The rule of law implies that every person is subject to the law, including persons who are lawmakers, law enforcement officials and judges. In this sense, it stands in contrast to tyranny or oligarchy, where the rulers are held above the law. When justice exhibits itself, there is evident wave trend of deliverance that distresses and overwhelms the oppressor, whilst it relieves the oppressed.

This has the following characteristics: fairness, impartiality, equity, honesty, integrity, uprightness, and truth. These create an atmosphere of aligning uneven things to build a peaceful and fruitful ecosystem amongst all people.

"He guards the paths of justice and preserves the way of His saints" (Proverbs 2:9).
Justice starts by seeing your neighbor as God sees him or her through His eyes of God's love. "Love your neighbor as you love yourself". All people are created in the image of God, and no one was made in the image of the devil or for

the devil.

"He that loves his brother abides in the light, and there is none occasion of stumbling in him. **But he that hates his brother is in darkness, and walks in darkness, and knows not where he goes, because that darkness has blinded his eyes**" (1 John 2:10-11).

Therefore, it is mandatory upon all believers to act in love and pursue justice on behalf of the oppressed.

"By this we know that we love the children of God, when we love God, and keep His commandments. **For this is the love of God, that we keep his commandments: and His commandments are not grievous**" (1 John 5: 2-3).

Then, as you have experienced freedom through the Love of God which brought you redemption and salvation for free, pursue freedom on behalf of others? As the LORD has been merciful to you, please be merciful to that person also through your acts of love: not in words but in truth.

"If a man say, I love God, and hates his brother, he is a liar: for he that loves not his brother whom he has seen, how can he love God whom he has not seen? And this commandment have we from him, that he who loves God love his brother also" (1 John 4:20-21).

This is your true worship and divine reverence to the most righteous LORD of lords the omniscient Judge. If the LORD God is "Your Worship", then it means whatever He commands you to do you shall do, and whatever way He divinely orders your steps by His Law you shall walk in uprightness and maintain justice.

It is with this code of law embedded into one's heart that judgment merges in, for whatever your spirit knows even your tongue can decode it in some ways as Jesus said;

"For by your words you shall be justified, and by your words you shall be condemned" (Matthew 12:26, 37).

It is without doubt then, that whosoever walks in love walks in righteousness, and would not desire to oppress others, because they have the Love of God within them which is without numeric nor a calculator, and gives generously. This love is patient. Love is kind. Love does not envy. Love does not boast. Love is not proud. Love does not dishonour others. Love is not self-seeking. Love is not easily angered. Love keeps no record of wrongs. Love does not delight in evil, but rejoices with the truth. Love always protects. Love always trusts. Love always hopes. Love always perseveres. Love does not parade itself. Love never fails.

When ruled by this Supreme Law of Love, your love will cause you to remember that you have offended or owe your brother or sister, and will not give you rest until you do justice to the matter before he or she cries to the judge and appeal against you as Jesus said:

"Therefore if you bring your gift to the altar, and there remembers that your brother has something against you; leave there your gift before the altar, and go your way; **first be reconciled to your brother, and then come and offer your gift**" (Matthew 5:23-24).

Your love should make you humble enough to appeal, and plead for forgiveness from the one you offended, even before you arrive in court before the judge as Jesus said:

"Agree with your adversary quickly, whiles you are in the way with him; lest at any time the adversary deliver you to the judge, and the judge deliver you to the officer, and you be cast into prison" (Matthew 5:25-26).

Your love is not proud, and so you can personally fix your marriage through it and do justice to those divorce papers as long as it is still in the will of the LORD, and that is, whilst your spouse still remains undefiled as Jesus said, "It has been said, whosoever shall put away his wife, let him give her a writing of divorcement:

"But I say unto you, that whosoever shall divorce his wife, except for the cause of fornication, causes her to commit adultery: and whosoever shall marry her that is divorced commits adultery" (Matthew 5:31-32).

The law of love within your heart should help you to think good thoughts of others, and to desire to good things for them rather than oppressing them as Jesus said:

"Therefore all things whatsoever you would that men should do to you, do even so to them: for this is the Law and the prophets" (Matthew 7:12).

Love will lead you to divine perfection where you reach a point of great strength, to overcome the evil spark of offence and persecution. The Holy Spirit will come in as your intercessor to defend your cause and innocence even in court.

"Whenever you are brought to trial, take no thought beforehand what you shall speak, neither do premeditate: **but whatsoever shall**

be given you in that hour that you must speak: for it is not you that speak, but the Holy Spirit" (Mark 13:11).

Instead of revenge, your love overcomes your enemies and brings his or her offence to justice by subduing his or her heart as Jesus said: "Give to him that ask you, and from him that would borrow of you turn not yourself away.

You have heard that it has been said, Thou shalt love thy neighbor, and hate your enemy. But I say unto you, love your enemies, bless them that curse you, do good to them that hate you, and pray for them which despitefully use you, and persecute you; that ye may be the children of your Father which is in heaven: for he makes his sun to rise on the evil and on the good, and sends rain on the just and on the unjust.

For if ye love them which love you, what

reward have ye? Do not even the publicans the same? And if ye salute your brethren only, what do you more than others? Do not even the publicans so? Be ye therefore perfect, even as your Father which is in heaven is perfect" (Matthew 5:42-48).

If the law of the LORD abides in you, then your love will lead you into many upright walks of life. You will obey and love God and set your heart to attaining the life of His.

Thus in all your prosperity as He blesses your just character, your love will not cause you to delight in flamboyance to show off your wealth to those who have none because the command of love says:

"Love not the world, neither the things that are in the world. If any man love the world, the love of the Father is not in him. For all that is in the world, the lust of the flesh, and the lust of the eyes, and the pride of life, is not of the Father, but is of the world. And the world passes away, and the lust thereof: but he that doeth the will of God abides forever" (1 John 2:15-17).

When truly led by the law of love, you will know how to apply that same law and do justice with someone else's possession. Then you will not withhold back what does not belong to you, but your love will give it to the owner.

See the following scenario Jesus responds to a question that relates giving right to possess to an owner of property:

"Tell us therefore, What do you think? Is it lawful to give tribute unto Caesar, or not?

But Jesus perceived their wickedness, and said, Why tempt ye me, ye hypocrites?

Show me the tribute money. And they brought unto Him a penny.

And He said unto them, Whose is this image and superscription?

"They say unto him, Caesar's. Then said He unto them, **Render therefore unto Caesar**

the things which are Caesar's; and unto God the things that are God's.

When they had heard these words, they marveled, and left Him, and went their way" (Matthew 22:17-20).

CHAPTER 7

JUDGES (DELIVERERS)

As stated in the previous chapters, the law and the standard plays a vital role in ensuring justice, and equity both in the spiritual and the physical world.

However, the law and the standards are not self-operational, but they need the services of a judge and that of an intercessor.

In the world today, every jurisdictions has judges. In the light of God's Law, judges are very important in every civilization and people to maintain justice.

There is a need to restore judges to the original value and role they played to society according to the Godly statutes, so that justice may be accorded to all without prejudice.

Without the intercessional role and power of the judge, people live in discord with unresolved conflicts that heighten to complicated crimes and unbearable kinds of oppression like terrorism, witchcraft, and Satanism, apart from falsely accusing one another, persecution, stealing, corruption, and killing each other for all the hateful and selfish reasons.

WHAT IS A JUDGE?

A judge is a public official vested with the authority to hear, determine, and preside over legal matters brought in a court of law. Judges attend to litigations between plaintiff and the defendant.

According to the Bible, judges were men and woman of God who were appointed with the Spirit of God to bring order against feud between two parties. The judges had understanding of the Law of the LORD God which was given by Prophet Moses. The *Book of Judges* revolves around a succession of judges. A judge is a righteous deliverer.

THE ORIGIN OF THE APPOINTMENT OF JUDGES

Judges can be traced back to Israel through the Holy Bible where we see the first nation that was legislated by a well constituted Law designed by the LORD God. It may not be certain by scriptures that Moses's father in law was inspired by the LORD God to tell Moses to appoint judges who could help him in judging the people.

However, we know by the number of men (seventy) who were imparted by the LORD God through the anointing that He had put on Moses, that Moses had enough unction to carry the burden of interceding in the whole assemble. Moses was a *"double edged sword"* prophet –operating as a judge (evaluator of the law), and an intercessor (mediator to pass judgment or sentence between the right and the wrong).

Nevertheless, the bottom line is that, the LORD God allowed Moses's father-in-law's advice to appoint judges to be approved, for it was indeed relevant to governing people. Then, an instruction concerning the official appointment of judges throughout the generations was issued, and that is how judges came to being.

"You shall appoint for yourself judges and officers in all your towns… and they shall judge the people with righteous judgment" (Deuteronomy 16:18).

THE NEED FOR JUDGES

Lawlessness and oppression called for a need for judges. Notice that, those judges did not rise at their own accord to judge and deliver the people from the oppression of their enemies. However, they manifested themselves as angelic ministers after they were appointed by the LORD God, to judge and execute sentence according to His Spirit (Angel of Justice).

In the following verse, we notice a judge rising up and stands for the justice of the Children of Israel against their adversary.

"When the sons of Israel cried to the LORD, the LORD raised up a deliverer for the sons of Israel to deliver them, Othniel the son of Kenaz, Caleb's younger brother. The Spirit of the LORD came upon him, and he judged Israel" (Judges 3:9).

It is clear therefore, that judges were appointed by the LORD God as an answer to an outcry to Him by the people who pleaded against the oppression by the enemy. Therefore, apart from their judicial function to intercede, judges were also assigned by the unction of the Holy Spirit to execute judgment on the nations that came against Israel to oppress the people and loot their properties.

For which, most of the time, these oppressions happened because Israel had sinned against the LORD God by falling in love with other gods (idols made of wood and stones).

According to the records of the Bible, the Children of Israel were accustomed to falling short over and over again with regard to this matter, meaning that they were rebellious against His Law and the greatest commandment which says:

"Thou shalt love the LORD thy God with all your heart, and with all thy soul, and with all thy might" (Deuteronomy 6:5). (See the Book of Judges Chapter 2, verses 13 to 23).

A HEAD OF STATE MUST ALSO APPLY JUSTICE

Samuel the Seer operated as a full time judge and an intercessor at the same time. He was appointed by God, and he took over his position and judged the nation Israel with the divine unction to intercede. The man of God was also well versed with the Law of God. He had spent most of his early years learning the Law of God through Priest Elli.

Afterward when he became aged, his sons judged with partiality, and injustice increased in Israel. The people felt oppressed, then the elders of the nation gathered to him and asked for a king that would judge them like the other countries. The book of Acts 13:20 records that God gave judges to the children of Israel to judge the people, and they served for four hundred and fifty years, until Samuel the prophet (last judge).

Thereafter, the duties of judges in Israel were dominated by kings. King Saul became the first king to judge Israel. His reign was supposed to last forever, but he unfortunately missed the mark of the commandment of the Spirit of the LORD (Angel of Justice). King Saul judged with partiality a treason case which the LORD God had charged against Amalek. This same case was pending the execution of a death sentence for more than 450 years. God had been waiting for the right judge, and when King Saul was put on the throne, the LORD brought the case to remembrance.

However, God was prejudiced by King Saul in this matter. King Saul let live Agag the king of the Amalekites, and he did not do justice to the whole matter. Then he went to roast the fat steers which he had illegally plundered for himself during his judgment against Amalek.

How did the Amalekites commit injustice? Amalek attacked the strugglers who were weak in the wilderness.

At that time, these Children of Israel were

still very young, and they did know how to war. It displeased the LORD to see the giant nation of Amalek squash the baby nation Israel in the wilderness for that matter.

And the LORD said unto Moses, 'Write this for a memorial in a book, and rehearse it in the ears of Joshua: for I will utterly put out the remembrance of Amalek from under heaven. And Moses built an altar, and called the name of it Jehovah Nissi: For he said, because the LORD hath sworn that the LORD will have war with Amalek from generation to generation' (Exodus 17:14-16).

With that said therefore, a head of state may also play the role of a judge. He must be righteous to judge people: "A king who sits on the throne of judgment winnows out all evil like chaff with his eyes" (Proverbs 20:8).

In the book of kings we see judges in the days of King Solomon: "Solomon spoke to all Israel, to the commanders of thousands and of hundreds and to the judges…" (2 Chronicles 1:2).

CONTEMPORARY JUDGES

The same word "judge" is, however, used in modern Israel to denote judges whose function and authority is similar to that in other modern countries. In the world today, judges are often appointed by the head of state.

King Jehoshaphat appointed judges in the land of Israel in all the fortified cities of Judah, city by city" (2 Chronicles 19:5).

In many jurisdictions judges may be appointed for life, so that they cannot be removed by the executive. However, in non-democratic systems, the appointment of judges may be highly politicized and they often receive instructions on how to judge, and may be removed if their conduct does not please the political leadership.

It is a common practice in some jurisdictions to elect judges in a political election. A professional judge is required to be legally educated. Generally, one requires a degree of Juris Doctorate in order to qualify to be a judge, and also, significant professional experience is often required. However, a volunteer judge, such as an English magistrate, is not required to have legal training and is unpaid for his or her services.

ADDRESSING A JUDGE

Above all these, remember that the Lord Jesus is the Lord of lords, which means He is the one who is above judges. You should address Him as, "My Lord, and My God", and He will reveal to you every hidden secrets in any case you are dealing with.

"The disciple is not above his master, nor the servant above his lord. It is enough for the disciple that he be as his master, and the servant as his lord" (Matthew 10:24).

The Lord Jesus does not have a problem with you being addressed as lord as it is in heaven. The Law came from God to keep His people in unity and peace, and so He placed judges to watch all this for Him and so we have judges all over the world.

In whatever your case may be, consider it in your mind that it is very important to address a judge in a polite manner whilst making your defenses in court: graciously and respectfully knowing that Jesus Christ the judge of judges is in control.

Addressing a judge impolitely is a serious offence against the LORD God. It is as good as passing judgment upon yourself. To contempt a judge, is to reverse mercy until you plead for pardon where pardonable,

Addressing a judge varies from country to country. Let us look at how they are addressed in some few countries around the world.

Judges are commonly addressed as "My Lord" or "My Lady" and referred to as "Your Lordship" or "Your Ladyship."

In Germany, judges are addressed as "Mister Chairman" and "Madam Chairwoman", or as Hohes Gericht, which translates as "High Court".

In the Netherlands, presiding judges of either gender are, in writing only addressed (edelachtbare) "Your Honor" for judges in the Court of First Instance (edelgrootachtbare) "Your Great Honor" for justices in the Court of Appeal, and (edelhoogachtbare) "Your High Honor" for justices in the High Council of the Netherlands Supreme Court.

In Portugal, presiding judges during trial are addressed as (Meretíssimo Juiz) when a man or (Meretíssima Juíza) when a woman meaning, "Most Worthy Judge" or as (Vossa Excelência) "Your Excellency" when not specifying gender.

In Spain, magistrates of the Supreme Court, magistrates and judges are addressed to as "Your Lordship" (Su Señoría); however, in formal occasions, magistrates of the Supreme

Court are addressed to as, "Your Most Excellent Lordship."

In the Courts of England and Wales, Supreme Court judges are called Justices of the Supreme Court. Justices of the Supreme Court who do not hold life peerages are now given the courtesy style "Lord" or "Lady."

When a Justice of the High Court who is not present is being referred to they are described as "Mr. /Mrs. /Ms. Justice N." In legal writing, the post-nominal letter "J" is used to denote a Justice (male or female) of the High Court: for example, Smith J.

Masters of the High Court are addressed as "Master". Insolvency and Companies Court judges in the High Court are addressed as "Magistrate". Circuit judges and recorders are addressed as "Your Honour". Circuit judges are referred to as "His/Her Honour Judge N". In writing, this title is occasionally abbreviated as "HHJ" or "HH Judge N", but not in legal writing.

District judges and tribunal judges are addressed as "Sir/Madam". Magistrates are usually still addressed as "Your Worship" in much of England. Magistrates are also addressed as "Sir/Madam".

THE POWERS OF A JUDGE

Judges and intercessors form a part of the government of the Kingdom of Heaven. The cause of injustices oppresses the people of God the Father of all creation, hence a righteous judges who fear the LORD must be appointed over the people of God. Judges are expected to judge the land with righteous standards, and great accountability.

"For God will bring every act to judgment, everything which is hidden, whether it is good or evil" (Ecclesiastes 12:14).

Judges are required to have good moral character, for example they must have no history of crime. The powers of a judge are checked by higher courts such as appeals courts and supreme courts.

"Therefore thou art inexcusable, O man, whosoever thou art that judges: for wherein thou judges another, thou condemns thyself; for thou that judges does the same things" (Romans 2:1).

A righteous judge should not fear to pass deserving judgment to chastise the wicked: **"If there is a dispute between men and they go**

to court, and the judges decide their case, and they justify the righteous and condemn the wicked" (Deuteronomy 25:1-2).

The powers of judges vary widely across different jurisdictions. In some jurisdictions, the judge's powers may be shared with a jury. In inquisitorial systems of criminal investigation, a judge might also be an examining magistrate. Here are some powers of a judge:

1. Oversee Court Proceedings

The presiding judge ensures that all court proceedings are lawful and orderly. Judges also supervise that trial procedures are followed, in order to ensure consistency and impartiality and avoid arbitrariness.

"If a malicious witness rises up against a man to accuse him of wrongdoing, then both the men who have the dispute shall stand before the LORD, before the priests and the judges who will be in office in those days. **The judges shall investigate thoroughly, and if the witness is a false witness and he has accused his brother falsely"** (Deuteronomy 19:16-21).

2. Investigating and Documenting

Judges must be able to research and process extensive lengths of documents, witness testimonies, and other case material, understand complex cases and possess a thorough understanding of the law and legal procedure, which requires excellent skills in logical reasoning, analysis and decision-making.

"If a slain person is found lying in the open country in the land which the LORD your God gives you to possess, and it is not known who has struck him, then your elders and **your judges shall go out and measure the distance to the cities which are around the slain one"** (Deuteronomy 21:1-2).

A judge is an eye of God with regards to the law of a nation and that of God. He is also His voice with regards to His judgments to sentence and render justice to the oppressed.

Therefore, a judge must look into every litigation with reverence fear of God for he or she will "give account to Him who is ready to judge the living and the dead" (1 Peter 4:5).

3. Passing a Ruling (sentencing/Judgment)
The main fact finder is the jury, and the judge will then finalize sentencing. Nevertheless, in smaller cases judges can issue summary judgments without proceeding to a jury trial.

In continental Europe, there is no jury and the main fact finder is the judge, who will do the presiding, judging and sentencing on his own. A judge must hear all the witnesses and any other evidence presented by the barristers or solicitors of the case, assesses the credibility and arguments of the parties, and then issues a ruling in the case based on their interpretation of the law and their own personal judgment.

4. Monitors the Execution of Judgment

Judges exercise significant governmental power. They can order police, military or judicial officials to execute searches, arrests, imprison, garnish, detrainment, seizures, deportations and similar actions.

Judges may work alone in smaller cases, but in criminal, family and other significant cases, they work in a panel. In some civil law systems, this panel may include lay judges.

In the earthly courts, judges are often assisted by law clerks, and lawyers in legal cases and by bailiffs or security. In the spirit realm judges are assisted by Angels of the LORD God which understand the law —the Angels of Justice and they pursue any hiding criminal.

RULES REGULATING JUDGES
(ACCORDING TO THE BIBLE)

- Always remember that, justice is a godly order and fear God.
- Never preside over a case of your interest
- Recuse yourself from judging a case that involves people who are close to you.
- Pass judgment without partiality.
- Do not pass sentence without investigating the cause of offence and complaint.

"Hear the cases between your fellow countrymen, and judge righteously

between a man and his fellow countryman, or the alien who is with him" (Deuteronomy 1:16).

- Petition God concerning sins of the people involved in a case for some cases have a sense of animosity and bestial practices which must be banned from communities. **"The righteous care about justice for the poor, but the wicked have no such concern"** (Proverbs 29:7).

- Ensure justice for the afflicted. **"Do not pervert justice; do not show partiality to the poor or favoritism to the great, but judge your neighbor fairly"** (Leviticus 19:15).

- Keep righteous judgments. "In a dispute

they shall take their stand to judge; **they shall judge it according to My ordinances** they shall also keep My laws and My statutes in all My appointed feasts and sanctify My Sabbaths" (Ezekiel 44:24).

- Do not pervert justice even by taking bribes. **"Give justice to the weak and the fatherless; maintain the right of the afflicted and the destitute,"** (Psalm 82:3).

- Defend the orphans and widows. **"Learn to do good; seek justice, correct oppression; bring justice to the fatherless, and please the widow's cause"** (Isaiah 1:17).

- Judge all wicked practices without

partiality. **"Do not pervert justice; do not show partiality to the poor or favoritism to the great, but judge your neighbor fairly"** (Psalm 33:5).

- Seek the face of God, and pray for a revival of the Law of God. **"In a certain city there was a judge who did not fear God and did not respect man.** "There was a widow in that city, and she kept coming to him, saying, 'Give me legal protection from my opponent....he granted" (Luke 18:2-8).
- **"Follow justice and justice alone"** (Deuteronomy 16:20).

CHAPTER 8

DECREES AND DECLARATIONS

A declaration is a statement spoken in good faith through the power of a tongue in favor of someone against an oppressive negative situation. It is given out by a man or a woman standing in the authority.

"You will declare a thing and will be established for you" (Job 22:28).

A decree is synonymous with the word judgment. It is a declaration stating a final verdict about a matter after judging that matter.

There are evil verdicts decreed by the enemy against God's people. However, the verdicts passed by God's intercessors through utterance or writing justifies His people who are oppressed, and these overrides the evil verdicts.

"Your sins are forgiven, pick up your mat and go."

CONDITIONS OF A JUDGMENT OR DECREE

A decree is often a final determination, but there are also interlocutory decrees. A final decree fully and finally disposes of the whole litigation, determining all questions raised by the case, and it leaves nothing that requires further judicial action; it is also appealable.

An interlocutory decree is a provisional or preliminary decree that is not final and does not fully determine the suit, so that some further proceedings are required before entry of a final decree.

"Also I have made a decree, that whosoever shall alter this word, let timber be pulled down from his house, and being set up, let him be hanged thereon; and let his house be made a dunghill for this" (Ezra 6:11).

A decree or judgment is usually not appealable, although preliminary injunctions by federal courts are appealable even though interlocutory.

"And when **the king's decree which he shall make shall be published throughout all his**

empire, (for it is great,) all the wives shall give to their husbands honor, both to great and small" (Esther 1:20).

A decree or judgment may be binding and subject to its duration for example: forever, i.e. a marriage or eternal punishment of demons in hell, or it may be for a duration of period to serve a legal purpose or chastisement until the consummation of sin i.e. a prison term.

Most decrees made by word of mouth or written down may leave the declarer with a guilty conscious, and trouble if made in haste. This is because, a person who is in such high authority to pass judgment or decree must do it with an oath of truth.

That means, he or she is not allowed to change his or her mind after the decree has been passed, but wait for its fulfillment. That's the rule of truth.

Therefore, every matter must be carefully

judged first, before a ruling is decreed and declared. The decree must be constructed to fulfil a good end without intentions to oppress.

"Woe unto them that decree unrighteous decrees, and that write grievousness that they have prescribed" (Jeremiah 5:22).

DECREES PASSED BY A RULER

Executive orders, which are instructions from a head of state to the executive branch of government, are decrees in the general sense in that, they have the force of law. Although they cannot override statute law or the Constitution and are subject to judicial review. Governors of individual states may also issue state executive orders.

"So they established a decree to make proclamation throughout all Israel, from

Beersheba even to Dan, that they should come to keep the Passover unto the LORD God of Israel at Jerusalem: for they had not done it of a long time in such sort as it was written" (Chronicles-2 30:5).

THE IMPORTANCE OF A JUDGMENT

Decrees are very important for establishing a matter. The creation of the universe and all that is in it was through the decrees of the LORD God after carefully examining the earth which was without form. Then He made decrees by His word of mouth, and all the good things were formed and they began to function according to His decree. All that was created was given judgments or statutes to set their limits.

"He gave to the sea His decree, that the

waters should not pass his commandment: when he appointed the foundations of the earth" (Proverbs 8:29).

DECREES PASSED BY AN INTERCESSOR

The judge must always liaison with the Holy Spirit concerning matters, before judging cases. This is very important, so that you do not condemn people who may be innocent. Unlike in the case of a rare wisdom of Apostle Paul where he showed in his teaching, that he is expressing his own mind over a situation, but not the mind of the Holy Spirit he said: **"I, not the Lord, say'**…(1 Corinthian 7:12).

That became: Thus says Paul, but not, *"thus says the LORD."* After you have said everything good or evil about a matter from your position of standing, know that the LORD still has a better say. Be careful then, rather than saying: *"Thus says the LORD"*, when actually it's your mind saying, but the LORD did not decree anything: you must say: **"I say" or "I think"**.

Then, indeed if there is no sin over the person you are declaring your good thoughts upon, your light will shine and all shadows of darkness will despair. This is because, as a believer you have the power to bind and lose things even by your tongue.

However, when sin prevails in the heart of the person you are declaring in favor of, nothing good will happen that you declared. But, the consequences of sin which is judgment from above will manifest, because the LORD God is a just God. He does not pass out a decree of judgment against a person without looking at the matter in truth, and judging it according to the Law that He has given.

"God is not a man that he should lie; neither the son of man, that he should recuse Himself: He has said it, and shall He not do it? He spoken, and shall He not fulfil it? **Behold, I have received commandment to bless: and He has blessed; and I cannot reverse it.** He has not found iniquity in Jacob, neither has He seen perverseness in Israel" (Numbers 23:19-21).

Every man or woman in a position of authority does not need to wait for the word to come from heaven in order to make a decree against demons. That word is in you as you have been given power and authority to judge every cause of evil in the name of Jesus. Therefore, you cannot look on when a person is harassed by evil sprites.

However, there are situations that need's an intercessor to wait for the actual decree from God in order to challenge and judge some demons and evil sprites for some of them are deliberately sent by the LORD as a means of executing His judgment.

"…the Spirit of the LORD departed from Saul, **and an evil spirit <u>from the LORD</u> troubled him**" (1 Samuel 16:14).

And the LORD said unto him, "Wherewith? And he said, I will go forth, and I will be a lying spirit in the mouth of all his prophets. **And He said, Thou shalt persuade him, and prevail also: go forth, and do so.** Now therefore, behold, **the LORD has put a lying spirit** in the mouth of all these thy prophets, **and the LORD has declared evil against you**" (1 Kings 22:22-23).

INTRICACY OF DECREES

The difficult part of a prophetic declaration is that, an undiscerning judge may ignore the actual mind of God, and His judgment concerning the matter. Thus, the declaration does not produce the decreed outcome. The smoke does not usually fuss without a burning fire.

"Without wood a fire goes out; without a gossip a quarrel dies down" (Proverbs 26:20).

Therefore, like in that case of king soul and his distressing spirit which was sent by the LORD God; and king Ahab and his false prophets who received a lying spirit also from the LORD so that, they may deceive Ahab to fall into a snare that eventually killed him.

Some evil spirits do not come to war and attack some people without a cause, but God is behind them —meaning that their oppression is an active judgment from God.

In such cases no intercessor could prevail in making a declaration to oppose. Such a declaration to combat or oppose God's judgment becomes a deadly lie, and that's what it is. It is like covering rotten and muddy food with white cloth.

But before you make a decree or a declaration, go to the root cause of the problem. Check the cause of the strange fire before casting water over it or try to escape the smoke.

Otherwise, some fires burning sources become more volatile when quenched with water. Then, they cause an explosion which may take away your own life, and yet you were trying to help. Many people are suffering today: in sickness, problems, delays, deaths, this or that.

Most of the time, it is because of the consequences of a sin that is haunting them from their past. That very sin which you have never repented or confessed before God causes you trouble.

They move from pastor to prophet; and from witchdoctor to spiritists, but come back with no stable solution. Even after many hours of prayers that are binding, breaking and losing, the devils tormenting a sinful person who resist to repent become steel-clad.

Check the base area of the life of the person you are declaring good health and prosperity to: Are there sins he or she did not confess before God or he or she needs to apologize to somebody offended?

Did he or she repent truly and the cause of sin judged in his or her life? Because, although some people confess their sin, but they do not repent from within their hearts?

Saul said unto Samuel, **"I have sinned: for I have transgressed the commandment of the LORD, and your words:** because I feared the people, and obeyed their voice. Now therefore, **I pray you pardon my sin, and turn again with me, that I may worship the LORD"** (1 Samuel 15:24-25).

King Saul confessed before Samuel that he had sinned, but he had not repented from his sin. How he had been pursuing to kill the righteous and execute the priests during the cause of his judgment by a distressing spirit shows that he never had repented.

A BLESSING ALWAYS RESISTS AN EVIL DECREE

The decree of a blessing over your life attracts a

blessing when you stand right with God.
Balaam was sent by an evil ruler to go and declare and decree a curse over the children of Israel, but he could not even try it:

"Surely there is no enchantment against Jacob, neither is there any divination against Israel" (Numbers 23:23).

A decreed blessing reverts and rejects a curse to get in contact with it. Check your life, what type of events dominates you? What kind of people are around you, and why? Keep away from people who declare negative and despising decrees over your life when you know you are right with God. They are evil enchanters sent by evil spirits to declare a curse over the works of your hands.

"Whoever says to the guilty, "You are innocent," will be cursed by peoples and

denounced by nations. But it will go well with those who convict the guilty, and rich blessing will come on them" (Proverbs 24:24-25).

Keep yourself in the company of people who will encourage you and admonish you with the word of God and never oppose God's declarations but consider carefully what He is saying to you and why.

RESULTS OF RESISTING GOD'S RULINGS

Let us look at more of the examples below of very hard tried declarations in the Bible, and spot the difference between a judgment and a declaration that comes by the LORD to accomplish God's judgment and the one that comes to oppose it. Read the following scriptures very carefully: (Jeremiah 27,28).

AN ILLEGITIMATE DECLARATION

There's a Prophet in the book of 1 Kings 22. Whilst about 400 prophets of Israel prophesied, and declared through a lying spirit in favor of the King of Israel who enquired from them. The king Ahab hated prophet Micaiah because he did not declare in his favor but what God showed him.

"As the Lord lives, whatever the Lord says to me, that I will speak" (1 Kings 22:14).

Indeed, what he spoke came to pass. Some "man of God" speak what they think will fit the situation or event —they pacify the sinful minds. And you wonder why people are not imparted with change after that. No one repents from grave sin, and no one is healed after their decrees.

True healings follow to confirm the message of the Gospel, but not the exhorter's pacifying words meant to sooth the pangs of God's judgment on a sinful person. No matter how hard you try to sooth a sinful man or woman, he or she will never repent. Then his negative case will become worse as Jesus said:

"No man also sews a piece of new cloth on an old garment: else **the new piece that filled it up takes away from the old, and the rent is made worse.**

And no man puts new wine into old bottles: else the new wine does burst the bottles, and the wine is spilled, and the bottles will be marred: **but new wine must be put into new bottles"** (Mark 2:21-22).

THE LORD'S VERDICT IS FINAL

When the LORD God's verdict has been passed, His judgment is executed by spiritual bodies and entities that cannot be understood or seen easily with the necked eye; and cannot be explained by the human mind. Here are examples of incidents:

"For the Lord will pass through to smite the Egyptians; and when He sees the blood on the lintel and on the two doorposts, **the Lord will pass over the door and will not allow the destroyer to come in to your houses to smite you**" (Exodus 12:23).

"**He sent upon them His burning anger, Fury and indignation and trouble, A band of destroying angels**" (Psalm 78:49).

And God sent an angel to Jerusalem to destroy it; but as he was about to destroy it, the Lord saw and was sorry over the calamity, and said to the destroying angel, **"It is enough; now relax your hand."**

And the angel of the Lord was standing by the threshing floor of Ornan the Jebusite. Then David lifted up his eyes and saw the angel of the Lord standing between earth and heaven, with his drawn sword in his hand stretched out over Jerusalem. Then David and the elders, covered with sackcloth, fell on their faces" (1 Chronicles 21:15-16).

"For the Son of Man is going to come in the glory of His Father with His angels, **and will then repay every man according to his deeds"** (Matthew 16:27).

WHEN JUDGMENT IS FAIR

As a Judge, make sure you have judged in righteousness for the oppressed, and sentenced the oppressor in righteousness, and you have not done the opposite. Chastisement relevant to a sentence, and of a just measure according to the full measure of offence is necessary to leave room for mercy.

Correct the soul with fair judgment, so that he or she may repent from his or her wickedness and return to the good image which God created. Unless the guilty truly deserves judgment by a death sentence, review the matter, so that you are not guilty of condemning to death one who is supposed to be sentenced with a light sentence, or is innocent.

That law of judgment by death was cancelled through the New Law of the love and mercy of God.

Therefore, judge the cause of killing, stealing and destroying with impartiality and give a sentence that is rather equal to death rather than a sentence of killing by killing. That would take us back to the old Mosaic Law where we would get an eye for and eye. What about a car for a car, or a wife for a wife, or a shoe for a shoe, or mob justice for a community offender? No ways!

Judgment is not about the replacement of things taken by the adversary. He or she did not borrow it, or nor was it given under pledge to him or her. Therefore, judgment is a harsh divine retribution and ruling by a judge, compelling the adversary to cover damages, repay, or restore, and face punishment for the wickedness of breaking the law. Here is an example of what happens after a person is found guilty:

"Men do not despise a thief, if he steal to satisfy his soul when he is hungry; **but if he be found, he shall restore sevenfold; he shall give all the substance of his house** (Proverb 6:30-31).

DISCERN YOUR JUDGMENT

The Law of God and the Spirit of Justice coexist. That is why a judge must consult the LORD about any matter before applying the law, and passing right judgment.

The case of Jesus before Pilate is a very good example. You may have to remember that until the wife of Pilate called Pilate aside and revealed to Him about what she was shown by the Spirit concerning the innocence of Jesus against all the charges that were levied against Him, Pilate would not judge fairly, but would have condemned the innocent, so as to satisfy the evil desires of the Jews.

Where there is the Spirit of God, there is truth, justice and equity. Those led by the Spirit of justice know that they must consult Him concerning any matter before they pass verdicts.

This was also a good practice that Moses as an intercessory prophet followed. It is through him where we see the first well drafted Law of God that governed people successively for generations. During his days, he sought the face of the LORD concerning every case that involved two parties, or one party and God. Here we find him telling someone:

"Stand still that I may hear what the LORD will command concerning you" (Numbers 8:8).

Imbalanced truth is injustice, perversion of the law, and oppression of the innocent. God values righteousness more than sacrifice:

"To do righteousness and justice is more acceptable to the LORD than sacrifice" (Proverbs 21:3).

The judges who are with the Spirit of the LORD are *Intercessory prophets (Interceders)*, and they have the unction to intercede. The first judges who were appointed to serve under Moses the prophet had an impartation of the Spirit, and could judge.

The LORD took that unction from Moses and placed it upon the newly appointed seventy judges. Discernment and wisdom is needed to see when God Himself is judging His people; or when the earthly standards must be applied to judge people on earthly matters, between themselves. And so is it –The **Heavenly Father's Law.**

The first Holy Law was given through

His Prophet Moses, and passed on to the Judges, prophets, priests, and kings. In many instances, the Pharisees and the teachers of the Law tested Jesus with matters of people who were accused of breaking the law to see if He could properly judge as a prophet. Let us look at two cases which were brought before Jesus to judge:

JUDGMENT OF THE WOMAN CAUGHT IN ADULTERY

"As he was speaking, **the teachers of religious law** and **the Pharisees** brought a woman who had been caught in the act of adultery. They put her in front of the crowd" (John 8:3).

Now, when a case is presented before a judge, witness is obligatory, and so, the lawyers presented their witness. Testimony given by the teachers of religious law:

"Teacher," they said to Jesus, **"This woman was caught in the act of adultery.** The Law of Moses says she be stoned. *What do you say?"*

They were trying to trap him into saying something they could use against him, but Jesus stooped down and wrote in the dust with his finger. They kept demanding an answer, so he stood up again and said,

"All right, but let the one who has never sinned throw the first stone!" Then he stooped down again and wrote in the dust.

When the accusers heard this, they slipped away one by one, beginning with the oldest, until only Jesus was left in the middle of the crowd with the woman. Then Jesus stood up again and said to the woman;

"Where are your accusers? Didn't even one of them condemn you?"

"No, Lord," she said.

And Jesus said, **"Neither do I. Go and sin no more."**

As the scriptures fulfilled: **"None is righteous not even one, for all have sinned."**

After judging all impure spirits —the causes of sin and sickness, Jesus always told the delivered, *"Go and sin no more."*

Conclusion of Matter: the accused woman was acquitted, and her case dismissed by Jesus —the Intercessor.

THE CASE ABOUT AN INHERITANCE JUDGED

"Teacher, tell my brother to divide the inheritance with me." But, He said to him, *"Man, who made Me a judge or arbitrator over you?"* **"Take heed and beware of covetousness, for one's life does not consist in the abundance of the things he possesses"** (Luke 12:15).

The young man had committed the sin of covetousness as stated in the law:

"You shall not covet your neighbor's house; you shall not covet you're your neighbor's wife, nor his male servant, nor his female servant, nor his ox, nor his donkey, nor anything that is your neighbor's" (Exodus 20:17).

Conclusion: The young man was found

guilty of breaking the law. Case dismissed with a warning –by Jesus the Intercessor.

JUDGING THE EARTH

The journey still continues as there is still a greater judgment day awaiting all humanity. That's where all people will account before God for all the evil works that they have done as foretold by John:

"Then I saw thrones, and they sat on them, and judgment was given to them" (Revelation 20:4).

"But why dost thou judge thy brother? Or why dost thou set at naught thy brother? For we shall all stand before the judgment seat of Christ. For it is written, "As I live, says the Lord, every knee shall bow to me, and every tongue shall confess to God. So then every one of us shall give account of himself to God.

Let us not therefore judge one another anymore: but judge this rather, that no man put a stumbling block or an occasion to fall in his brother's way. I know, and am persuaded by the Lord Jesus, that there is nothing unclean of itself: but to him that saw anything to be unclean, to him it is unclean. But if your brother be grieved with your meat, now do you walk charitably? Destroy not him with thy meat, for whom Christ died. Let not then your good be evil spoken of: (Romans 14:10-16). Stay true to your purpose!

CHAPTER 9

PREJUDICE

The topic of Justice is not complete until we address the issue of inequality, uneven-handedness or prejudice. One may blame the contemporary courts for prejudice, but prejudice is a bloodline issue imbedded in a person who does not have love. Through this book, you have learned through precept by precept until you found out where love comes from, and how to acquire it, so that you may do what is right to others. Before prejudice may be found in the world's judicial courts, it had first lingered at home amongst family members where it tormented some of them.

On its way to the court, it was revealed to strangers and visitors —those who are not part of the family or country or city. It is not supposed to be so! Prejudice is exhibited mainly through the way how one treats others with contempt, and makes them feel unworthy of anything good or to become anything good. Here is a simple example: "If a brother or sister is poorly clothed and lacking in daily food, and one of you says to them, "Go in peace, be warmed and filled," without giving them the things needed for the body, what good is that?" (James 2:15-17).

Before prejudice arrived in the hospital, it was first exhibited by a parent at home who treated one child or a set of children with partiality over the other. In the book of Luke chapter 16 verse 19-31), the Lord Jesus tells a story of the judgment of a rich man who treated a beggar with prejudice. And only for the act of prejudice against a human being this rich man was sent to hell, but the LORD consoled the beggar in paradise, and he is no longer a beggar.

In this life, it is heartening to see the poor and needy moved by the LORD God from their poverty to a way of life that builds their dignity and self-esteem. The needy and poor suffer prejudice and contempt a lot of times from the eyes of those who are able.

A needy or poor person is always looked upon with suspicious eyes as though he or she is a thief and might get away with some goods. That is why a person who looks poor and is poorly dressed, his or her acquaintances first looks at his or her shoes, and that makes them to decide where to sit him or where to room him or her to sleep.

"Listen, my beloved brothers, has not God chosen those who are poor in the world to be rich in faith and heirs of the kingdom, which he has promised to those who love him? But you have dishonored the poor man.

Are not the rich the ones who oppress you, and the ones who drag you into court? Are they not the ones who blaspheme the honorable name by which you were called?" (James 2:5-7). The act of blowing trumpets to the world whenever you do your charitable deeds to the poor and needy has a great element of prejudice. To be poor and needy affects the self-esteem of the one is such a situation.

He or she does not like it. In fact, if we are to put it in simple terms we would say; the needy and poor fool ashamed about their situation such that, they do not wish for everybody to know that they are poor. Therefore, when you come to help them, do not bring everyone but come yourself and share your love gifts so that they may bless the LORD your God, their God. Because, your giving is actually a sign of your love for God and His people.

Let the receiver of your gift be led by gratitude to openly bring your name to memory and thank you, upon realizing how your gift or help has moved them from need, and poverty to a better life. Showing yourself in public as you give alms to the needy, and bringing the media to ask them to give a word of thanks for your help and gifts is prejudice.

Although they may do it because you have already put them on the spot, but their hearts grieve, and regret being in need or why they are poor. A gift is a private parcel between the giver and the receiver. If it is not private, then it is an advertisement. Take it from the words of the Lord Jesus who treated no one with prejudice:

"Take heed that you do not your charitable deeds before men, to be seen of them: otherwise you have no reward of your Father which is in heaven.

Therefore when you give your alms, do not sound a trumpet before thee, as the hypocrites do in the synagogues and in the streets, that they may have glory of men. Verily I say unto you, they have their reward. But when you give alms, let not your left hand know what thy right hand does: That your alms may be in secret: and your Father which sees in secret, Himself shall reward you openly" (Matthew 6:1-4).

"ALL ARE EQUAL BEFORE LORD"

Justice is the nature of and heartbeat of the Lord Jesus. "For the LORD your God is God of gods, and Lord of lords, a great God, mighty, and awesome, **who shows no partiality, nor takes reward:** He does execute the justice for the fatherless and widow, and loves the stranger, in giving him food and clothing" (Deuteronomy 10:17-18).

Before the eyes of the LORD God, all people are equal and should respect one another equally. Some of the Angels despised mankind, and considered them lower than they because, mankind was created out of clay, whilst angels were created out of fire. But the LORD God disapproved them. He uplifted the despised spirit of man and addressed humankind as Elohim (mighty one) saying,

"You are gods; and all of you are children of the most High God" (Psalm 82:6).

If the creator sees His people as mighty ones or gods, then it is a great offence before Him to despise, or treat with contempt, or look down on anyone of them for whatever reason, or to treat a person in a way that would make him or her feel undermined or disregarded as a human being like in these prejudiced questions:

"Can any good thing come out of Nazareth?" (John 1:46).

Others were saying, "This is the Christ." Still others were saying, **"Surely the Christ is not going to come from Galilee, is He?"** (John 7:41).

Each time you come across a person who is trying to deal with a low self-esteem, know that someone is responsible for that torture, and the LORD will not delay to bring His justice to the offended. As in one occasion Peter the Apostle opened his mouth and said:

"Truly I understand that God shows no partiality (Acts 10:34).

The Lord Jesus walked the talk by practicing impartiality and did justice to all things. He advocated against prejudice many times, whilst He practiced compassion towards all people without making sport of them or the background.

"Therefore all things whatsoever you would that men should do to you, do even so to them: for this is the law and the prophets" (Matthew 7:12).

Although being the Son of God, but Jesus was often times addressed as the son of man. This made it easy for every soul to relate with Him whilst also a Son of God. Your rank does not matter to God, what matters to Him is how you treat other people.

If you walk humbly and seek not after your own glory or selfish interest, then you would not treat the image of God with contempt or handle any person's issue with prejudice. But you would listen quietly, observe, ponder about causes and concerns, and try how you can bring resolutions and comfort.

"He has told you, O man, what is good; and what does the Lord require of you, **but to do justice, and to love kindness, and to walk humbly with your God?"** (Micah 6:8).

The selfless lifestyle of the Lord Jesus gave hope to the hopeless when they perceived that, He experienced the same life, and viewed it with the same spectacle that was sized for all eyes of humankind. Thus being a Son of God, would on behalf of humankind fix all ails of discomfort to life by His spiritual authority and power.

"There is neither Jew nor Greek, there is neither slave nor free, there is no male and female, for you are all one in Christ Jesus"

(Galatians 3:28).

Prejudice is the language of segregation amongst families, people, and nations. It is marked with distinguishable codes that can easily be seen from a distance ranging from: The color of skin; location; language; educational background; wealth; association; health; age; gender (male or female according to God's creation before perversion), status (grading others), fashion, profession and religion: **"those who say, 'Keep to yourself, do not come near me, because I am holier than you!'** (Isaiah 65:5).

The Lord Jesus also suffered prejudice on account of His power and authority as a Son of God, and the people who believed in Him were prejudiced by religious men as it is today. Here is an example:

Then came the officers to the chief priests and Pharisees; and they said unto them, **"Why have you not arrested him?"**

The officers answered, **"There is no man who has ever spoken like this man."**

Then answered them the Pharisees, **"Are ye also deceived? Have any of the rulers or of the Pharisees believed on him? But this people who do not know the law are cursed"** (John 7:45-49).

This last statement here carries a sense of prejudice against the people.

CHAPTER 10
JUDICIAL PREJUDICE

Whenever the law societies and advocates of human rights put an emphasis on rights protection of a particular group or gender of people, the general outcome obviously becomes prejudice. In these days where the contemporary courts are populated by corruption, acts of judicial prejudice and unfair conducts are common.

Partiality is the unfair bias or prejudice against a person or group over another.

"For the LORD sees not as man sees: man looks on the outward appearance, but the LORD looks on the heart" (1 Samuel 16:7).

Some offenders know very well that they are guilty of the offence, but they push for the case to reach before the judge, instead of seeking for the mercy of the offended.

This is because, some hope that they could change the statement and press a bribe button on the mind of the judge, so that he may judge the oppressed with partiality. In every litigation, there is always a winner and loser and according to the common law of adversary love always conquers.

However, there are proven instances where there are signs of losing a litigation due to the exhibited partiality of the judge. If this is true of the judge, then it is proper for the law to render any judgment ensuing as illegal.

ACTUAL PARTIALITY

Actual partiality is common where the judge is involved in the lawsuit or has a financial or other interest in the outcome of the litigation.

"Truly I understand that God shows no partiality, but in every nation anyone who fears Him and does what is right (justice) is acceptable to Him" (Acts 10:34-35).

Actual partiality results from the state of mind of the judge with regards to personal interests or the interest of family member in the outcome of his or her partial judgment. Where a judge is actually partial in a decision, then justice has not been done to the matter and it is deemed prejudiced. This issue must be addressed as soon as possible, notwithstanding the judge has some relationship with a persons involved in the lawsuit. The caution must be the realistic effect of the judge's interest which might influence the prejudiced outcome.

"My brothers, show no partiality as you hold the faith in our Lord Jesus Christ, the Lord of glory. For if a man wearing a gold ring and fine clothing comes into your assembly, and a poor man in shabby clothing also comes in, and if you pay attention to the one who wears the fine clothing and say;

"You sit here in a good place," while you say to the poor man, "You stand over there," or, "Sit down at my feet," have you not then made distinctions among yourselves and become judges with evil thoughts?" (James 2:1-4).

APPARENT PARTIALITY

The judge's conduct and the surrounding circumstances may ring the alarm of apparent partiality. Apparent partiality is seen when there is something in the judge's conduct or behavior towards one party.

During the court proceedings, it is right for a judge to intervene in the course of witness evidence to ask questions that would give clarity to the matter without giving the impression of acting as an advocate. Acts of hostility and rudeness to a Plaintiff gives an impression that the Judge's intercessions in the case may result to an unfair outcome.

Although the judge is not a party to the proceedings, and does not have an interest in its outcome, but this sign of favoritism gives rise to a suspicion that he or she will not judge the case in an impartial manner.

"But as he was discussing righteousness, self-control and the judgment to come, Felix became frightened and said, "Go away for the present, and when I find time I will summon you" (Acts 24:25).

A decision tainted by apparent prejudice means that justice is not observed in the litigation and is unlikely to be done. It is therefore appropriate to enquire whether the presiding judge knew of the matter as appearing to undermine his impartiality. If it is revealed that he or she had no knowledge of it, the jeopardy of its having influenced his or her judgment is eliminated and the appearance of possible partiality may be dismissed. If a ground for objection for apparent partiality is known, this should be raised at the soonest possible juncture and the judge may recuse himself or herself.

APPARENT PARTIALITY CASE IN THE BIBLE

Think about this scenario of the case of Herodias the wife of Herod who hated John the Baptist, and the partiality of King Herod in handling this matter (Mark 6:18-28).

King Herod knew that John was innocent. He was in the right position of authority to resist the demand for the head of John. Nonetheless, because he loved Herodias his wife he could not humble himself to ask wisdom from God, so that He might plainly tell the daughter of Herodias that the head of John which she was asking for was not part of his estate and kingdom, and he did not own it, but John owned his own head.

Thus concerning the request for the head of John, it is advisable to make that request from John himself at a personal level and see if he would grant it. Instead, Herod allowed his relationship to abuse and control his authority in order to kill an innocent man who spoke the truth according to their law.

FALSE ACCUSATION

In these days, as Jesus said many will be offended, and will betray one another.

It has become a common thing to drag one another to court, even for matters which could have been resolved outside the court by the two parties which have indifference.

Hatred these days feels good to see another fellow banked in prisons. Therefore, they create false accusations against one another with a pile of written papers of fabricated evidence, farfetched to baffle the undiscerning judge.

"But whoever is angry with his brother without a cause shall be in danger of judgment" (Matthew 5:22).

Some lawyers and judges receive bribes, so that they may pervert justice in cases which are created to torture another person. Then the outcome of the case becomes **unfair justice**. The Spirit of justice declares: "God stands in the congregation of the mighty; **He judges among the gods. How long will you judge unjustly, and justify the wicked person?**

Defend the poor and fatherless: do justice to the afflicted and needy. Deliver the poor and needy: rid them out of the hand of the wicked" (Psalms 82:1-4). It is an unfortunate thing to find a prayer house dominated by talebearers who pollute intercession teams with invalid stories about people.

As a result, some prayer interceders do

not discern the allegations, but instead they pass decrees that bind an innocent person with evil. Mighty one, that is against the work of the Holy Spirit.

A large bunch of information presented to you as an intercessor or a judge, does not prove that the accused is guilty of the allegations until that information is tried and tested through proper investigated findings.

False accusations has always been common even in the religious circles where some develop a sense of insecurity about another clergyman. The strangest thing is that, many take a stand by every accusation they have fabricated.

The Jews once rose up and made false accusation against Paul the Apostle and presented him to the judge. He took his defense and cried out, **"Neither can they prove the things whereof they now accuse me"** (Acts 24:13).

Now therefore, an intercessor or a judge is not supposed side with accusations against any persons, and neither is he supposed to point fingers even after finding evidence. He or she must not slander or gossip any person based on the crimes they are accused of. But, an intercessor and a judge is a man or woman of God moving in righteousness to judge for the people of God and ensure justices upon all created things even the soil itself as this is a command from the LORD God.

"Thou shalt not wrest the judgment of thy poor in his cause. Keep thee far from a false matter; and the innocent and righteous slay thou not: for I will not justify the wicked.

And thou shalt take no gift: for the gift blinds the wise, and perverts the words of the righteous. Also thou shalt not oppress a stranger" (Exodus 23:1-4).

DEFAMATION OF CHARACTER IS PREJUDICE

In recent years, there are leaders and ordinary people who have faced defamatory of character after being falsely accused, and put in stocks without fair justice. Even after being acquitted from a false allegation, most courts rarely issues public statements of refrain for defamatory after the accused is proven innocent, there is scarce public apology to remedy the damages of the character of the person smear campaigned.

As a result, the unjustified when they come out to the society, they are prejudiced and bound with red tap known as *"controversial"*, *"scandalous"*. This has proven to work for the adversary as it hinders people from accepting that tainted person believed to be guilty.

However, the kingdom of God is still advancing, we have several intercessors who have this lordship unction to rule the nations in righteousness, and these are the hope to those who are hopeless who are oppressed by the cords of prejudice.

There are men and women who are able to hear the Holy Spirit, as He tells them what judgment they must give to the families or brethren who have cases against one another.

"Shall God not avenge His own elect who cry out day and night to Him, though He bears long with them? "I tell you that He will avenge them speedily" (Luke 18:8).

Truth must prevail against lie in order to judge the evil and set captives free. Mercy remains to plead for the compassion of the LORD by the people who repent.

"Justice and judgment are the habitation of thy throne: mercy and truth shall go before

thy face" (Psalm 89:14).

Whenever a lie is involved in a case no matter how much truth is in that case, the lie makes it to be judged against the accused. There you find the LORD of Justice taking sides with the accused because you have presented lies to strengthen your case before the LORD. In any case, you will find both you yourself and your offender harshly judged by God and both of you losing your case. Tell the truth as it is without painting it colors to make it appealing before the LORD.

CHAPTER 11

THE INTERCEDER

As we have looked at the matter of justice, we begun by tackling it from both the spiritual and physical point of view. We now shift further with the issue of justice, and the role of judges. Now, we dwell in the celestial realm where all things are established as the Lord Jesus prayed.

"Our Father in heaven, Hallowed be your name. Your kingdom come. Your will be done on earth as is in heaven.

Give us this day our daily bread. And forgive us our sins; as we forgive those who sin against us. Lead us not into temptation; but deliver us from evil. For Yours is the Kingdom, the power and the glory, forever and ever Amen."

WHAT IS AN INTERCEDER?

According to the Biblical law, judges were authorized by God to be His righteous law watchers, so that they might judge between the right and the wrong.

This role of judging between the wrong and the right is called intercession, and the judge is called the intercessor.

In the spiritual terms, the same anointed judge who also arbitrates is addressed as *lord*, or an *intercessor prophet*. "**…for he is a prophet, and** he shall pray for you, and you shall live" (Genesis 20:7).

The intercessor prophet is a person who is given authority by God to make appeals in prayer and to pass decrees or judgment against oppressive powers and evil principalities on behalf of the oppressed.

"He that is spiritual judges all things, yet he himself is judged by no man" (1 Corinthians 2:15).

THE ROLE OF THE INTERCEDER

The important role of an intercessor in a nation is to watch for harmony and officiating a national leader, who must then appoint sub-leaders.

A national leader is first officiated by the LORD God in the spirit realm before he or she is commissioned by oath according to the state law.

"And the LORD said to Samuel, Hearken unto their voice, and make them a king" (1 Samuel 8:22).

As a mediator, the intercessor seeks justice and harmony between the offender and the oppressed before God may pass a verdict. In the scriptures, we find the Lord Jesus working as a judge and an intercessor at the same time. That is why He is called the Messiah (Anointed One, synonym Christ).

"Neither is there salvation in any other: for there is none other name under heaven given among men, whereby we must be saved" (Acts 4:12).

Although the Lord Jesus has the authority to pass judgment on devils, He also has mercy to forgive sin. He has authority to deliver the oppressed from the cords of oppression, and save the unpardonable from condemnation by His name.

"If any man hear my words, and believe not, *I judge him not*: for *I came not to judge the world, but to save the world"* (John 12:47).

An intercessor who has received from God the unction to function like Christ Jesus also stands as a watcher to judge the devil and his works, and ensures that God's standard is preserved. For as Jesus Christ is doing in heaven **"even at the right hand of God, who also makes intercession for us"** (Romans 8:34), so are the intercessory prophets on earth.

As an intercessor and a judge, he or she stands in the position of the LORD the God of Justice and declare judgment from the LORD according to the accurate verdicts inspired by the Holy Spirit.

"Likewise the Spirit also helps our infirmities: for we know not what we should pray for as we ought: but the Spirit Himself makes intercession for us with groaning which cannot be uttered. And **He that searches the hearts knows what is the mind of the Spirit, because He makes intercession for the saints according to the will of God**" (Romans 8:26-27).

UNANSWERED BY THE LORD?

The rule of intercession is to decree justice to the oppressed and sentence the oppressor. The work of an intercessor is more than kneeling down to pray. There are codes of ethics that governs the intercessor in the line of duty.

As an intercessor, understand why some intercession prayers return unanswered by God, whilst it may take a few seconds for some cases to be vindicated. An intercessor arbitrates for the oppressed before the LORD God according to what is lawful, or is in His Law, or in His will as Apostle John explained:

"This is the confidence that we have in God, that, if we ask any thing according to His will, He hears us: If we know that He hear us, whatsoever we ask, we know that we have the petitions that we desired of Him.

"If any man see his brother sin a sin which is not unto death, he shall ask, and God shall give him life for them that sin not unto death. **There is a sin unto death: I do not say that he shall pray for it. All unrighteousness is sin: and** there is a sin not unto death."

Meaning that, the intercessor's appeal on behalf of the offender who has committed a sin whose condition of judgment from God is a death sentence, may not get a positive answer on behalf of the offender (1 John 5:15-17).

In other words, interceding outside the final ruling of God is asking Him what is not in His will or is outside His Law. Therefore, He does not grant that petition but lets His ruling to stand. Secondly, when you pray, pray with understanding! If you are not sure or very clear about the oppression of the enemy as presented by the oppressed, you will not be able to pray with understanding, and your petition will not make sense to the LORD, and you will be unlikely to receive your answer.

Remember that, prayer is an entreaty or an appeal expressing your desire, hope, wish to the LORD. Therefore, make it always clear and firm in your words. Imagine that your child comes to your living room and cry out, *"Food, food, food"*. What you would do is to go and give him or her food. But upon taking the food, the child still cries out, *"food, food, food"*.

That will make you upset, but if your child cries out for food, and explains what kind of food he or she wants, then as a parent, you would joyfully prepare that kind of food for your child whilst he or she waits. Or imagine that you are a judge, and a woman comes in the court before your judgment seat, and hysterically crying, *"Set me free, set me free"*. Won't you command the marshals to carry her outside until she calms down and explain her trouble very well, so that you may give her justice?

When the blind cried out, "Son of David have mercy on us", they expressed their appeal to the Lord Jesus whilst following Him, and revealing that they were in desperate need for vision.

The Lord Jesus said asked them, **"Do you believe that I am able to do this?"**

They said unto him, **"Yea, Lord."**

Then touched he their eyes, saying, According to your faith be it unto you. And their eyes were opened; and Jesus strictly charged them, saying, See that no man know it (Matthew 9: 28 -30).

You see, a cry out followed by a clear expression brings a spontaneous answer to your prayer. Do not just go about crying, but cry and finish. Calm down, and then speak your emotions to the LORD in words that He may understand.

"I cried to You, O LORD; and unto the LORD I made supplication" (Psalms 30:8).

There are people who have been crying

over an issue for some years, but they still have no answer, because they have never seriously prayed. However, they had always remembered to cry about it, and believed that God hears their cry. It is like putting a blame on the LORD. Yes, the LORD hears your cry, and He feels your heart, but He is only waiting for you to cheer up before Him and make a clear appeal about the matter. If you are crying, how will the Holy Spirit tell you that actually the cause of your calamity is the sin which you have never confessed?

"Learn to do well; seek judgment, relieve the oppressed, judge the fatherless, and plead for the widow. Come now, and let us reason together, said the LORD: though your sins be as scarlet, they shall be as white as snow; though they be red like crimson, they shall be as wool. If you be willing and obedient, you shall eat the good of the land: But if you refuse and rebel, you shall be devoured with the sword: for the mouth of the LORD has spoken it" (Isaiah 1:17-20).

PRESENT YOUR URGENT PETITION TO THE LORD

The Bible records many incidents in the Bible where people who were judged unfairly made urgent appeals to God.

"The LORD is gracious and full of compassion" (Psalms 111:4).

He does not turn a blind eye, nor a deaf ear to the outcry of the afflicted who cry upon Him for justice. Mordecai, Esther and all the Jews who were exiled under king Ahasuerus, under the Kingdom of Persia fasted for three days to make urgent appeals against their decreed annihilation. The execution of the king's decree to kill the Jews was only a few days away; and if they kept silent they would have all died, and today we would have no Jews through whom also Jesus was born.

Abraham stood as an intercessor to arbitrate and appeal in the presence of God on behalf of the righteous who were in the regions of Gomorrah and Sodom, so that God may acquit them from the offences of the people of the land whose verdict for judgment was release to be executed, (see Genesis 18).

Angels of execution were already on the way when Abraham made this urgent appeal for Lot and his family to the LORD of Justice. "But Abraham still stood before the LORD. He came near and said;

"Would you also destroy the righteous with the wicked?" (Genesis 18:23).

The people in Gomorrah and Sodom were charged with acts of homosexuality and pervasion of justice amongst other things. They used to abuse strangers and take by force people's possessions. When you study carefully the case of Gomorra and Sodom, you will realize that Lot having learned the ways of the LORD through Abraham, was trying to install righteous norms amongst the people of that land.

It was Lot who took a stand and intercede to the LORD for the upright, against the inhabitants of Gomorrah and Sodom. Nonetheless, being a foreigner there, Lot had it very difficult to judge the people, and on the day of God's judgment they vented out against Lot's righteous judgments and said:

"This one came in to stay here, and **keeps acting as a judge**; now we will deal worse with you than with them" (Genesis 18:9).

But unfortunately, they did not know that now angels had been sent to execute the judgment against them, with tangible evidence which they had themselves. The intercessions of Lot had reached God and He said;

"Because the outcry against Sodom and Gomorrah is great, and because their sin is very grave, **"I will go down now and see whether they have done altogether according to the outcry against it that has come to Me; and if not I will know"** (Genesis 18:21-22).

Many this present times have been moved by the Spirit of faith to present their prejudiced cases before the LORD, and He answered them. For those who have offended others and their apology is not accepted, also have a room in the court of heaven where you may plead for mercy before the LORD.

The petitions and supplication of a nation that is charge with sin by the LORD come before the LORD and as everyone turns from his evil way, He shows mercy and reverse His judgment. The Holy Spirit within you becomes imparts you with the anointing to intercede. Through Him your inner being pleads for your justice directly to the Father in Heaven. With the Holy Spirit in you, you are able to judge every evil thought, and temptation of the devil, by putting it under subjection. There are many occasions in the bible where urgent appeals were petitioned to God concerning issues which pertains to loss, life and health and welfare. You can also follow the same way and petition God concerning your urgent case for:

- **Healing and death reversal:** When King Hezekiah was told that he must put his house in order because he will die. He turned to the wall and petitioned God. Isaiah was sent him with a new ruling from God which acquitted Hezekiah from the former verdict where God had judged that he must die. He was granted 15 more years of good health instead of death.

- **Resurrection from the dead:** When Lazarus was sick, his sister made an urgent appeal to Jesus to come and heal him. However, when Jesus went there, Lazarus was about 4 days in the tomb, and Jesus resurrected Him according to the request of their first petition.

- **Deliverance from the oppression of demons:** The father of the epileptic boy who could not be delivered by the disciple went to make an appeal to petition Jesus to rescue him. And Jesus casted out the demon from the boy.

THE CONDITIONS OF AN APPEAL IN A PRAYER PETITION

1. Tell the LORD your Judge the matter in truth as it is, for he knows your heart.
2. You must have confidence and compassion in your petition knowing that you are asking God according to His will, and He hears your words. "Therefore the LORD waits to be gracious to you, and therefore he exalts himself to show mercy to you.

   For the LORD is a God of justice; blessed are all those who wait for him" (Isaiah 30:18).
3. Begin your petition by thanking God.
4. Mean the words you are saying, it is not about a skill of saying good words over a situation, but presenting the situation

to God, and appeal for His intervention from a true heart.

5. Say what you want the outcome of your appeal to be, and do not say words like, *"Lord if you will, heal me or bless me"*, that is a sign of lack of confidence in God.

6. Be straight to the point. *"Ask and you will be given"* Hold on to the Spirit of faith. "And if we know that He hears us, whatever we ask, we know that we have the petitions that we have asked Him" (1 John 5:15).

CHAPTER 12

THE UNCTION TO INTERCEDE

The unction to judge evil powers, oppressive territorial demons, and to deliver the people of the LORD God does not function at one's will. It takes a process that requires careful spiritual preparation for an interceder to receive this higher dimension of authority. The spiritual sharpening process produces a devout chastised character. A well-disciplined character forms a good quality personality that can endure hardships, and overcome the persecutions of the evil one without giving up.

A good character withstands strategic storms that are designed by Satan to oppose your prayer petitions to the LORD. The training of an interceder is more than the training of a military commander. A military commander on training may easily access his ration of food from his master. However, here the LORD your training master may even let you over to hunger, and need, as a means to train your character so that, you may remain humble and selfless. For this is the kind of a soldier He wants for this kind of office.

"May the God of all grace, who called us to His eternal glory by Christ Jesus, after you have suffered a while, perfect, establish, strengthen, and settle you" (1 Peter 5:10).

I had a vision of an angel of the LORD who spoke to me the same words in verse 9 saying, "Resist him (the devil), steadfast in the faith, knowing that the same sufferings are experienced by your brotherhood in the world." At that time I was experiencing a lot of hardship in my life. I was almost at the breaking point. Thanks be to the LORD, the Angel of the LORD picked me up, and strengthened my feeble knees even by that word.

My heart was also strengthened, and I moved on with life until I emerged in my destined realm with the Lordship unction to function with an out stream of wisdom. Every time I think that I have done the best, the LORD appears and always help me to do yet the best, for He is the most perfect God, who uplifts the simple to do the best. Unless you have personally experienced the saving power of God delivering you from hardship; you may not be able to know the meaning of deliverance, so as to deliver others. Here is an example of a very powerful intercession:

"Thus they provoked Him to anger with their inventions: and the plague broke in upon them. Then stood up Phinehas, and executed judgment: and so the plague stopped. And that was counted unto him for righteousness unto all generations for evermore" (Psalms 106: 29-31).

Until you learn how to endure trials and tribulations, you are not yet fit to pass the test to become a king who must reign with Jesus Christ in the heavenly places. The Lord Jesus decreed:

"He that overcomes, and keeps My works to the end, to him will I give power over the nations: And he shall rule them with a rod of iron; as the vessels of a potter shall they be broken to shivers: even as I received of my Father. And I will give him the morning star"

(Revelation 2:27-28).

With all that said, you have understood that, interceding is not for the proud and self-exalted, but it is for those who are chosen, humbled and elevated by the LORD.

The anointing to intercede comes with a responsibility from the Holy Spirit, and poured upon the humble chosen vessels of clay (people), so that they may function and bear much fruit for the praise and glory of God. This is the unction for ruling the nations on behalf of the LORD.

Whether you are a Prophet, Intercessor (Judge) or King. This unction carries boldness, and is regulated by the statute of the LORD God which says, ***"Do not fear."***

THE AUDACIOUSNESS THAT CAUSES THE UNCTION TO FUNCTION

Once appointed by the LORD to be lord, He gives you the Lordship unction to function and the scepter (rod) of ruling.

This Lordship anointing graces your presence with authority and divine virtues that evil powers, intruders, sabotage, and impostors cannot withstand. Instead, they bow in alarm and plead: *"Mercy my lord"*.

Therefore, you need to maintain boldness as the LORD also prompts you to believe, and remain fearless:

"Why fear? This very day I will begin to put the terror and fear of you on all the nations under heaven. They will hear reports of you and will tremble and be in anguish because of you" (Deuteronomy 2:25).

"Why should you suppose that God will cast you down before the enemy? For God has power to help or to cast down" (2 Chronicles 25:8).

When assigned by the LORD with this grace for ruling on wickedness, causes intense retaliation from the camp of the devil to erupt against you. This is a very sensitive realm of authority in the supernatural. Here you are entrusted with the deliverance, and freedom of nations, groups, and individuals. The LORD expects you to ensure justice to the oppressed, according to what is lawful, and which is also in the will of the LORD God.

Therefore, **"when men are cast down, then you shall say, There is lifting up; and the LORD shall save the humble person. He shall deliver the island of the innocent: and it is delivered by the pureness of your hands"** (Job 22:29-30).

You must always look to the Lord Jesus where all victories comes from, so that you may stand and watch in the Spirit of faith. Just as the Lord Jesus said; **"I am with you always."** After Jeremiah was told by God what He has made him to become to the nations, He gave him the same hope and there was never a day where God failed Jeremiah the prophet. This is what He said to Him:

"Today I have made you a fortified city, an iron pillar and a bronze wall to stand against the whole land against the kings of Judah, its officials, its priests and the people of the land. **They will fight against you, but will not overcome you, for I am with you and will rescue you, declares the LORD"** (Jeremiah 1:18-19).

If you are living your life according to the will of God, He promises throughout scripture to never leave you nor forsake you. Ask Him what His will is for you and learn to follow it with boldness.

"Be strong and courageous. Do not be afraid or terrified because of them, for the Lord your God goes with you; he will never leave you nor forsake you" (Deuteronomy 31:6).

It is very important to let the unction to intercede fully function in your life, so that you may perfectly accomplish your assignment to set every captives free.

It is through the boldness that comes by the anointing to intercede, that you may boldly rebuke every evil works of the devil as the scripture say:

"For this purpose the Son of God was manifested to destroy the works of Satan" (1

John 3:8).

As the mercy of the LORD remains forever, plead for the compassion of the LORD for mortals who repent from evil deeds to be expiated from their sins by the blood of Jesus. Pray that, evil men may be conveyed into the kingdom of God as new creatures.

Take time to mind your spiritual life and nature your relationship with the Lord Jesus. Refrain from searching out and pointing spots on the little children of God who are trying to pursue Gods standards but keeps on falling. If your prayer cannot help them to notice their dirty spots, gossiping them may paste their spots on you, and your lips become dirty as their garments are.

"You who are of purer eyes than to see evil and cannot look at wrong, why do you idly look at traitors and remain silent when the

wicked swallows up the man more righteous than he?" (Habakkuk 1:13).

Be bold as a lion! Boldness is not the rise of egos and arrogance as some reveal in their character. As a result, they despise the LORD's instructions, but boast about their mighty strength and powers. They begin to forget where the LORD has picked them from –thorn bushes and set them amongst lilies of the beautiful valley. Your boldness must be full of wisdom –*the fear of the LORD to follow all His instruction.* The boldness which is full of sin will not help you when the LORD turns His back on you (2 Kings 17:18). Boldness comes by the Spirit of faith to give you irresistible dominion over all paradigms on earth, so that you may access supernatural dimensions for the manifestation of great miracles to deliver the bound, *and that is what pleases God.*

"Therefore, they spent a long time there speaking boldly with reliance upon the Lord, who was testifying to the word of His grace, granting that signs and wonders be done by their hands (Acts 14:3).

You cannot exercise your God given authority without boldness. It is through boldness that you may approach the LORD and believe that, you have received what you asked Him for in prayer.

"I will bring him near and he shall approach Me; for who would dare to risk his life to approach Me?' declares the LORD" (Jeremiah 30:21).

Boldness stands against fears in violent confrontations, and causes evil powers and rulers of darkness to embargo.

"For God has not given us a spirit of

timidity, but of power and love and self-discipline" (2 Timothy 1:7).

"The wicked flee when no one is pursuing, but the righteous are bold as a lion" (Proverbs 28:1).

Boldness drives faith to manifest greater results.

"So that the manifold wisdom of God might now be made known through the church to the rulers and the authorities in the heavenly places. This was in accordance with the eternal purpose which He carried out in Christ Jesus our Lord, in whom we have boldness and confident access through faith in Him" (Ephesians 3:10-12).

Fear has no place in the life of a man or woman of God. By the name of Jesus Christ who lives in you, you've been given authority over fear.

If you're starting to feel anxiety or fear creeping into your mind, you can rebuke this in Jesus' name, and find peace in the Spirit of God that gives us His power, love, and self-discipline.

"When they had prayed, the place where they had gathered together was shaken, and they were all filled with the Holy Spirit and began to speak the word of God with boldness" (Acts 4:31).

WITHSTAND THE DEVIL

Under this unction, there is astounding backing by the Holy Spirit and an army of angels of the LORD. The Holy Spirit effects your voice to be heard, and your holy angelic presence felt by demons. Fear of the demons, and disobedience causes the unction of the Holy Spirit to stop flowing.

This provokes God to great anger, as it is more than what a master experience when his workers sabotage the business, and still expect to be paid for being employees of that company. Won't they be fired! God picks up cowards and transform them by His Spirit to be great judges for His glory. For then, these will always depend on Him, unlike the all-knowing people who are too confident about their knowledge.

"For you see your calling, brethren, how that not many wise men after the flesh, **not many mighty, not many noble, are called:** But God has chosen the foolish things of the world to confound the wise; and God has chosen the weak things of the world to confound the things which are mighty; and base things of the world, and things which are despised, has God chosen, yes, and things which are not, to bring to naught things that are: **That no flesh should glory in his presence"** (1 Corinthians 1:26-29).

Once transformed and anointed, you are expected to cower no longer. Instead, you become God's game changer. Therefore, the enemy is supposed to cringe down by the knees, and flee away from you, unlike in those days when you were not anointed.

As our Lord Jesus who came to intercede for the cause of the sinner, so are you placed on the seat of judgment and given a scepter to measure cases and judge without fear of man or demons.

As the following words were said to Him by the LORD God who sent Him to intercede, so He sends you, and speaks the same words to strengthen your spirit. As the Lord Jesus has judged evil powers, and so shall you do:

"The LORD said unto my Lord, sit at my right hand, until I make your enemies your footstool. **The LORD shall send the rod of your strength out of Zion: rule in the midst of your enemies.** Your people shall be willing in the day of your power, in the beauties of holiness from the womb of the morning: you have the dew of your youth.

The LORD has sworn, and will not repent, You are a priest for ever after the order of Melchizedek. The Lord at your right hand shall strike through kings in the day of His wrath. He shall judge among the heathen, He shall fill the places with the dead bodies; he shall wound the heads over many countries. He shall drink of the brook in the way: therefore shall He lift up the head" (Psalms 110:1-7).

As an intercessor in this realm of important spiritual authority, you will often times find yourself confronted or having to confront the evil powers, principalities, rulers and all deterring devices of Satan in reality, so that you may rescue the oppressed. To deliver the oppressed from the hands of devils and satanic agents, is like declaring war against Beelzebub and Hell itself. Be aware of their devised darts, and remain fortified with heavenly protection as Apostle Paul quickened the spirits of the Ephesian church by alerting them to:

"Put on the whole armor of God that you may be able to stand against the wiles of the devil. **For we wrestle not against flesh and blood, but against principalities, against powers, against the rulers of the darkness of this world, against spiritual wickedness in high places.**"

"Wherefore take unto you the whole armor of God that ye may be able to withstand in the evil day, and having done all, to stand. Stand therefore, having your loins girt about with truth, and having on the breastplate of righteousness; and your feet shod with the preparation of the gospel of peace;"

"Above all, taking the shield of faith, wherewith ye shall be able to quench all the fiery darts of the wicked. And take the helmet of salvation, and the sword of the Spirit, which is the word of God: **Praying always with all prayer and supplication in the Spirit, and watching with all perseverance and supplication for all saints;"** (Ephesians 6:11-18).

Fueled by the compassion of Christ, an interceder engages in issues of injustice, protecting the vulnerable, fighting for those held in oppression, walking alongside the wounded, and pointing them to the One who heals, restores and redeems.

Pursuing justice for the oppressed starts and continues with prayers. Fully understand that, this is Christ's battle but not our own. The fight involves time, and that means stepping out of your comfort zone, and persevering with patience until you see victory. It means walking in wisdom and not jumping in haphazardly or foolishly with aimless spiritual weapons.

The Lord Jesus leads the way, and you follow as He empowers you through the Holy Spirit. Withstand the Devil, and boldly engage in the fight for deliverance as prophet Jeremiah assured his soul.

"But the LORD is with me like a might warrior, so my persecutors will stumble and not prevail. They will fail and be thoroughly disgraced; their dishonor will never be forgotten"" (Jeremiah 20:11).

SEEK THE GUIDANCE OF HOLY SPIRIT

The intercessor may have to spend a lot of time in the Bible and praying to seek the LORD about right rulings in complicated matters. When bestowed with authority for territorial work, you are led by the Spirit of Justice declare a single sentence decree or one-word ruling after carefully discerning a matter about an oppression. The result of a righteous decree from the mouth of an anointed interceder is an instantaneous execution of judgment. It is the LORD of lords that stands beside you to accomplish all these greater works, but not your own strength.

"You shall make your prayer unto Him, and He shall hear you, and you shall pay your vows. **You shall also decree a thing, and it**

shall be established: and the light shall shine upon your ways" (Job 22:27-28).

Therefore, in order to become consistent as a judge or interceder, always have a constant contact with God through prayer, and be with the Holy Spirit. You need the Holy Spirit to help you to pray for the justice and liberation of the captives where ever they may be.

"In the days of Lord Jesus in His flesh, He offered up both prayers and supplications with loud crying and tears to the One able to save Him from death, and He was heard because of His holiness" (Hebrews 5:7).

It is unwise to quench the Holy Spirit by resisting His impulse to lead you to pray. When you ignore or resist the impulse of the Holy Spirit, it is treating Him with contempt. This is worse than your act of ignoring an urgent incoming phone call of a person, when actually you are in a right position to answer it.

The caller feels rejected, and might never call again because of that, until you return the call and explain why you ignored the call. Resisting prayer when asked by the Holy Spirit, means that you resist His prop or notice to have a conversation with you.

The sad part is that, you may return His call latter, but as said letter, your call or prayer to the Holy Spirit might be very late, and He may not return to you. Know then that, as an interceder you cannot access the Father directly without praying in the Holy Spirit in the name of the Lord Jesus. It is also impossible to hear and receive from the Holy Spirit without the authorization of the Lord Jesus and the Father. The Holy Spirit speaks and does what is approved by the Father and the Son. He does not do His own will. Always take heed and obey the voice of the Holy Spirit.

CHAPTER 13

THE ANGEL OF JUSTICE

You may be wondering if the LORD God in heaven overstep His power to intrude into human issues and disputes when there are human courts and judges set in place there on earth? If He did, there would be no perversion and injustice in the nations of the world. Although God is the creator of the universe, but He does not impose His power to control any earthly system.

He gave unto man the power to rule, and subdue the earth according to just means and with great accountability. The LORD is the God of order, harmony and peace. Therefore, order, peace and harmony is all that He expects man to exhibit in the earth. He tests man and allow earthly rulers rule their systems according to their heart desires, so that He may fully know their intentions.

"The LORD knows the thoughts of man, that they are vanity" (Psalms 94:11).

Therefore, whenever there is an outcry from the oppressed, and there is no intercessor to justly defend and judge the oppressor, that outcry for justice provokes the righteousness of the LORD God. He sends the Angel of Justice to look into the matter, and right here on earth, as the scripture says:

"The LORD also will be a refuge for the oppressed, a refuge in times of trouble" (Psalms 9:9).

Whenever there is human blood crying suit before the God of justice, He the LORD does not turn a deaf ear, but He stands up for the cause of their assassination to judge the assassin. Here are examples of incidents where the LORD came down to judge and delivered the oppressed without the use of earthly judges:

"The LORD said, **Because the outcry of Sodom and Gomorrah is great, and because their depravity is very grievous; I will go down now, and see whether they have done altogether according to the cry of it, which is come unto me; and if not, I will know**" (Genesis 18:20-21).

"And the LORD said, I have surely seen the oppression of my people ... by reason of their taskmasters; and have heard their cry for I know their sorrows; and I have come down to deliver them" (Exodus 3:7-8).

Now, understand that the LORD does not leave His throne in heaven to come down in person to attend to issues and troubles of human beings. He sends down an Arch Angel that is relevant to such matters, and that is the Angel of Justice from the Court of Heaven. This Arch Angel comes in the power of the name and authority of the LORD.

This is because in the first place He has given the earth unto man to govern it, He expects man to act right. But when man fails to do his righteous duties to maintain the light that God gave him, then the LORD comes in. A preacher once proclaimed, "Jehovah ufohlihle!" Meaning that, the LORD has made an entrance into fortified high towers of human abode unexpectedly, and without permission.

When the LORD is involved in a nation or amongst people in the like manner, then the case becomes very complicated for the ordinary judges who are in the local court. They cannot understand nor pass the right ruling over it.

"...He makes the judges of the earth as useless" (Isaiah 40:23).

This is because, no human can put his little hand on top of the hand of the LORD God to interfere with what He is doing. But once He puts His mighty right hand against what you are doing, that evil deed of yours immediately falls under the subjection of His power.

"He sent upon them His burning anger, fury and indignation and trouble, a band of

destroying angels" (Psalm 78:49).

In that case, you can only appeal to Him to lighten His heavy hand, so that it does not kill you. Although you would no longer have control over that evil deed of yours as long as His hand is busy dealing justly with it, but expect ashes in place of your evil glory. Yes the LORD's divine intercession brings forth true justice and deliverance.

"To set up on high those that be low; that those which mourn may be exalted to safety. **He disappointed the devices of the crafty, so that their hands cannot perform their plans. He takes the wise in their own craftiness: and the counsel of the forward is carried headlong.** They meet with darkness in the daytime, and grope in the noonday as in the night. **But he saves the poor from the sword, from their mouth, and from the hand of the**

mighty" (Job 5: 11-15).

If the educated judges are undiscerning, they would not see that a case has made a twist, and is lifted up to a spiritual dimension where it can no longer be judged and resolved by a learned human judge.

Such a case can only be judged by a judge who knows the times and has the unction to interpret the verdicts of the LORD God which are presented by the Spirit of Justice. That is what Moses the prophet did before Pharaoh and the Egyptians.

When the Jews were prejudiced in the realm of India, the LORD sent the Angel of Justice and deliverance from heaven to come and intercede through Esther and Mordecai. He helped them to fight for the justice of the Jews, and reverse the verdict to annihilate them, which was decreed in favor of their adversary. The king and Haman sat down to drink wine;

but the city Shushan was perplexed.

"And in every province, whithersoever the king`s commandment and his decree came, there was great mourning among the Jews, and fasting, and weeping, and wailing; and many lay in sackcloth and ashes" (Esther 4:3).

The people of God appealed to the LORD in heaven, and it did not take long, the reversal of the decree which was intended to annihilate all the Jews for selfish reasons was reversed.

THE DUTIES OF THE ANGEL OF JUSTICE

As the Father has given authority to His Son Jesus Christ to be Lord of lords, then the Lord Jesus assigns the Angel of justice to visit earth to access an outcry, and then judge.

"For as the Father has life in Himself; so has He given to the Son to have life in Himself; **and has given Him authority to execute judgment also, because He is the Son of man.** Marvel not at this: for the hour is coming, in the all that are in the graves shall hear His voice" (John 5:26-28).

Angels of Justice may suspend and subject to judgment any law that limit people to the sphere of lawlessness. They also suspend the corrupt universal laws that also govern people in iniquity in the name of power and wealth creation.

The LORD assigns the Angels to judge every oppressive laws of any people, and domicile. There are oppressive laws are set up in some countries, and other laws that promotes perversion before the eyes of the LORD. Such laws are a snare to judgment and an embarrassment to God. Thus, He always rescue His people who plead with Him whilst in bondage as it happened to Peter the Apostle who later testified and said:

"Now I know of a surety, that the Lord Jesus has sent His Angel, and has delivered me out of the hand of Herod, and from all the expectation of the people of the Jews" (Acts 12:11).

The Angel of justice proclaim verdicts and monitor the execution of judgment without fear nor favor of any man. He makes sure that those who nullify God's will by oppressing others are taken under judgment for the deliverance of justice.

"When justice is done, it brings joy to the righteous but terror to evildoers" (Proverbs

21:15).

The Angel of Justice's purpose has always been to keep devils in check, and delivering sentence to those who over-step their boundaries. He has been known to liberate the crying captives from the hands of wicked spirits, and cast the devils back into Hell. He separates the sheep from the goats, that is, the righteous from the lawless. He seats the righteous on the right, and the wicked on the left, and render to each person according to his or her deeds.

"...the LORD the Judge be judge this day..." (Judges 11:27).

According to the will of God, an Angel of justice may be found in the high court to help a judge understand a matter, so that he may judge fairly, and monitor that the judgment is executed according to what the LORD had projected as an answer to prayer.

"Seeing it is a righteous thing with God to recompense tribulation to them that trouble you; And to you who are troubled rest with us, when the Lord Jesus shall be revealed from heaven with his mighty angels, in flaming fire taking vengeance on them that know not God, and that obey not the gospel of our Lord Jesus Christ: Who shall be punished with everlasting destruction from the presence of the Lord, and from the glory of his power; (2 Thessalonian 1:6-9).

Imagine that you have been found guilty, and the LORD gives you a dream that tells you about how He will punish you for your evil deeds, but you do not understand the dream. Look for an interceder, and the Angel of justice will translate the verdict given through the strange language, to the language that may be understood. This is because, the Law has a language and terms that are not easy to understand with simple national or tribal language. And so, there are angelic tongues that proclaims mysteries about a judgment as in the following manner:

"Then the fingers of the hand were sent from Him, and this writing was written" (Daniel 5:22-24).

ANGELS EXECUTING JUDGMENT

Addressed as "Lord", the Angel of justice has the responsibility over the law. He renders judgment according to the law, and commandment of the LORD God. However, there are Angels which are responsible for the execution of the verdicts.

"The LORD is known by the judgment which He executes: the wicked is snared in the work of his own hands. The wicked shall be turned into hell, and all the nations that forget God. For the needy shall not always be forgotten: the expectation of the poor shall not perish forever. Arise, O LORD; let not man prevail: let the heathen be judged in thy sight. Put them in fear, O LORD: that the nations may know themselves to be but men" (Psalms 9:16-20).

Arch Angel Michael is head of the department of the defense Angels that executes judgment on the guilty. He is the law enforcer of the Supreme Court of Heaven. He and the defense angels executes the punishment of the wicked according to the measure specified by the verdict of the LORD.

They take instructions directly from the

LORD's Judgment table, and they are addressed as "Master". The angels of records serves them with timelines for executing judgment and delivering justice for the executing angels to act. Thus went out a hymn of invocation from the mouth of King David after he perceived that the LORD has assigned supernatural intercession in the case against his adversary. He sang the praise invocation to strengthen his faith and forecast in the just outcome of the judgment of the LORD. The same invocation gives an idea about what happens when Angels are involved in delivering justice to the oppressed:

"Let those be ashamed and dishonored who seek my life; Let those be turned back and humiliated who devise evil against me. Let them be like chaff before the wind, with the angel of the Lord driving them on. Let their way be dark and slippery, with the angel of the Lord pursuing them" (Psalm 35:4-6).

The arrival of Angel Michael in a country or place means that, that country's wickedness has been measured through the scales of justice in the court of heaven, and a verdict of the LORD concerning that high crime in that country has been passed, and can no longer be reversed. Here is an example:

"Then the Angel of the Lord went out and struck 185,000 in the camp of the Assyrians; and when men arose early in the morning, behold, all of these were dead (Isaiah 37:36).

Here is another example of an execution of Judgment: "That very night Belshazzar, king of the Chaldeans, was slain and Darius the Medes received the kingdom, being about sixty-two years old" (Daniel 5:30-31). "And immediately the Angel of the Lord smote Herod" (Acts 12:23).

The righteous verdicts gives power to the

Angels of judgment to execute judgment without respect of ranks of persons: evil leaders, kings, rulers, presidents, prime ministers, members of parliament, lawyers, headman, chiefs and wayward nations.

CHAPTER 14

COOPERATE WITH THE SPIRIT OF JUSTICE

A man stood opposite him with his sword drawn in his hand"" (Joshua 5:13). The High Court in heaven is under Justice Lord Jesus the Lord of lords, King of kings. There is a throne of judgment in heaven where the LORD of Hosts –Jehovah Sabaoth sits to judge and commission an army to go and execute judgments against His enemies in any realm or country or people.

The enemies of the LORD are those who oppress His people. Angel Michael is responsible over every head of the armies of the LORD to strengthen it on earth, so that they may fight the battles of the LORD. In Egypt, he was behind the release of the armies of all the animals, and the pestilence that tormented Pharaoh and the Egyptians when he resisted God's command to let His people go.

"Appoint a general against her, cause the horses to come up like the bristling locusts" (Jeremiah 51:27).

The evil one is always afraid to mention the angelic military with his tongue; instead he refers to them as *"hedge" or "protection"*. When Satan wanted to attack Job, he saw the military angels around Job, and his household and all that he had (Job 1:10).

As the bible say; **"The angel of the LORD encamps round about those who fears Him and he delivers them** (psalms 34:7).

Satan was given temporal power over Job, and the defending militant angels retired to heaven. Angel Michael is also responsible over the souls of man, and he holds them in high esteem and guards their blood against attacks of the enemy.

"Only do not lay your hand on his soul" (Job 1:12).
Thus, the human blood has supernatural blood soldiers which are subject to the Spirit of God. When these militant blood rebels the Spirit of God, the soul dies. The troops of soldiers that guard the body from sickness are called *the white blood cells*. So even though Job was

attacked on the outside, but his soul –the blood was intact until the warfare that was to test his character and faith in God was over.

Then, he was restored seven times more through God's order of recompense. His later days became greater than the former. The Lord God the Father of a creation gave all authority and power to Jesus His Son to judge all things. He is therefore your advocate, even to judge death itself.

"For the Father judges no man, but has committed all judgment unto the Son" (John 5:22).

It is not wise to despise and pervert justice of the LORD, because the LORD of lords may rise and come down to judge for His people who are oppressed, and then you may not even find a stand to make your appeal to Him. Fear God!

"But we are sure that the judgment of God is according to truth against them which commit such things. And think thou this, O man, that judges them which do such things, and does the same, that thou shalt escape the judgment of God?" (Romans 2:2-3).

VENGEANCE IS THE LORD'S HE VISITS EVERY SECRET

God sees the hearts and minds and will judge all men. We can have peace knowing that God's authority prevails above all and evil will be dealt with. The scriptures tells us that, vengeance belongs to the LORD God, and He will repay the evil one for all the evil He has done against a person. This promise has be tried, tested and proven to be true:

"Now is the end come upon thee, and I will send mine anger upon thee, and will judge thee according to thy ways, and will recompense upon you all your abominations. And My eye shall not spare you, neither will I have pity: but I will recompense your ways upon you, and your abominations shall be in the midst of you: **You shall know that I am the LORD. Thus says the Lord GOD; An evil, an only evil, behold, is come"** (Ezekiel 7:3-4).

"God will bring into judgment both the righteous and the wicked, for there will be a time for every activity, a time to judge every deed" (Ecclesiastes 3:17).

"For we know Him who said, "It is mine to avenge; I will repay," and again, "The Lord will judge His people" (Hebrews 10:30).

"But you must return to your God; maintain love and justice, and wait for your God always" (Hosea 12:6).

Whatever offence you commit in secret and hide the evidence, know that as long as it is against a fellow human being (your neighbor), the LORD already knows about it and it does not matter who you are.

"He reveals the deep things of darkness and brings utter darkness into the light" (Job 12:22).

The LORD will fully avenge on your behalf. But when you fight for yourself He stands afar, and watch the fight whilst He nods His head at your humiliating defeat. Do not take revenge, my dear friend, but leave room for God's wrath, for it is written:

"It is mine to avenge; I will repay," says the Lord. "For Me, the LORD, love justice; I hate robbery and wrongdoing" (Isaiah 61:8-9).

BE CAUTIOUS WITH THE RULES OF ENGAGEMENT

The danger with the involvement of the Angel of Justice is that, when you turn against God, and rebel or sin, He also turn against you and stand on the side of your enemy to watch him fight and overcome you, and this is what is happening in many countries today.

Whilst people are seeking for deliverance from an oppressive ruler or a condition, they kill, steal and destroy as a means to show their own strength and human power to overthrow instead of looking up to God.

"Do not say, I will recompense evil; but wait on the LORD, and he shall save you" (Proverbs 20:22).

"For the LORD is our judge; the LORD is our lawgiver; the LORD is our king; He will save us" (Isaiah 33:22).

A left hand over another left hand will never produce a right hand, but it still remains a left hand. Thus, Israel was defeated at Ai because they broke this rules of engagement, and as the LORD enlightens Joshua:

"Stand up! Why have you fallen on your face? Israel has sinned; they have transgressed my covenant that I commanded them, and they have taken some of what was devoted.

**"Indeed, they have looted and lied about it,

and they have put these things with their own possessions. This is why the Israelites cannot stand against their enemies" (Joshua 7:10-12).

Although the Angel of Justice presented himself to Joshua, he made it clear that he was not there to favor anybody, although God had specifically sent him to bring justice by judging the enemies of God whose measure of sin had become full. Take notice of the conversation between the Angel of Justice and Joshua the leader of the children of Israel.

Joshua went up to him and asked: ***"Are you for us or for our enemies?"***

"Neither", he replied, **"But as commander of the army of the Lord I have now come."**

Then Joshua fell face down to the ground in reverence, and asked him:

"What message does my Lord have for his servant?"

The commander of the LORD's army replied: **"Take off your sandals, for the place where you are standing is holy. And Joshua did so"** (Joshua 5:13-15).

There are many leaders today who forget that their strength and protection comes from the God of Justice. He bestows it on the arm of flesh, and may decide to judge the enemy without human hands. The LORD executes His judgment and saves either by many or by few. Never rely on the multitude of human soldiers therefore if you have lifted up your case of oppression by your opponent into the court of Heaven.

The LORD longs to be gracious the oppressed; therefore He will rise up to show you compassion. For the LORD is a God of justice.

Blessed are all who wait for him! People, you will weep no more. How gracious He will be when you cry for help! As soon as He hears, He will attend to your oppression as He said in His word:

"Listen to Me, My people; hear Me, My nation: Instruction will go out from Me; My justice will become a light to the nations. My righteousness draws near speedily, My salvation is on the way, and **My arm will bring justice to the nations.** The islands will look to Me and wait in hope for My arm" (Isaiah 51:4-5).

Plead for mercy so that your judgment may become lighter if in the course of the angelic interference you have broken some rules of engagement as many leaders and nations fall in default. Learn to know that angels are servants from the presence of God, and they are loyal to God as He expects you to be.

They serve you as you serve God, not when you serve yourself. When you don't serve God, they withdraw their services from you, and you serve yourself and fall. At a specific hour they retire to worship God at 5 P.M.

There, they deliver reports about your works and everything that you have done in that day, both the good and evil things. They do not forget to also report about your pride and rebellion if you have exhibited such character.

Angels plead with God never to return back a rebel who takes God's glory: That is one who boast about dominance and power over people who he makes subjects after the LORD has earned him victory and elevation.

These are main things that move Angels of the LORD to plead with God to never return to such a one as you. It was a very good thing for the children of Israel to have an angel that accompanied them. But there was an instruction given to Moses proving that it is not a simple thing to have an Angel coming from the presence of God, to abide with man. This was the instruction:

"Pay careful attention to him and listen to what He says. **Do not rebel against Him; because He will not forgive your rebellion, since my Name is in Him**" (Exodus 23:21).

Vagabond angels from the fallen group of angels can remain with people for a lifetime if they don't chase it away, in the Name of Jesus. But the angels sent from the presence of the LORD has heaven as their home. Therefore, these ascend and descend for a duration of specific time, to do their assignment, or just a visit which may last seconds, minutes, hours or days then they ascend.

Angels do not camp at a place for no reasons. And the camping angels may look like they are the same angels, but it is thousands upon thousands taking turns until their mission is done.

But, if it is the same angel following you year in and year out, ask him what is his name and what is his mission in your life and who sent him? Make sure otherwise you could be followed by a demon right there.

"Angels who did not keep their own domain, but abandoned their proper abode, He has kept in eternal bonds under darkness for the judgment of the great day" (Jude 1:6).

The angel who after wrestling with Jacob, blessed him and went back to heaven before it was 03.00 A.M. The time of the day had to be prolonged and sun made to stand still to give angels extra time to fight for the armies of Israel who were led by Joshua. At sunset, a shift of angels must return to worship God in Heaven.

SCRIPTURE REFERENCES ABOUT JUSTICE

JUDGE

The LORD **judge** between me and you (Genesis 16:5).

Then shall the trees of the wood sing out at the presence of the LORD, because He cometh to **judge** the earth (1 Chronicles 16:33).

For by fire and by his sword will the LORD **judge** all flesh: and the slain of the LORD shall be many (Isaiah 66:12).

Agree with your adversary quickly, whiles thou art in the way with him; lest at any time the adversary deliver thee to the **judge**, and the judge deliver thee to the officer, and thou be cast into prison (Matthew 5:25).

Judge not, that ye be not judged. For with what judgment ye judge, ye shall be judged: and with what measure ye mete, it shall be measured to you again (Matthew 7:1, 2).

Man, who made me a **judge** or a divider over you? (Luke 12:14).

...a **judge** who did not fear God (Luke 18:2).

Judge not according to the appearance, but **judge** righteous judgment (John 7:24).

You **judge** after the flesh; I judge no man. And yet if I judge, my judgment is true: for I am not alone, but I and the Father that sent me (John 8:15, 16).

I charge thee therefore before God, and the Lord Jesus Christ, who shall **judge** the quick and the dead at his appearing and his kingdom (2 Timothy 4:1).

JUDGES

Be wise now therefore, O ye kings: be instructed, ye **judges** of the earth (Psalm 2:10).

When their **judges** are overthrown in stony places, they shall hear my words; for they are sweet (Psalm 141:6).

"Kings of the earth, and all people; princes, and all **judges** of the earth: Both young men, and maidens; old men, and children: Let them praise the name of the LORD: for his name alone is excellent; his glory is above the earth and heaven (Psalm 148: 11-13).

I will restore thy **judges** as at the first, and thy counsellors as at the beginning: afterward thou shalt be called, the city of righteousness, the faithful city (Isaiah 1:26).

He makes the **judges** of the earth as vanity (Isaiah 40:23).

For the Father **judges** no man, but has committed all judgment unto the Son (John 5:22).

But he that is spiritual **judges** all things, yet he himself is judged by no man (1 Corinthians 2:15).

He that **judges** me is the Lord (1 Corinthians 4:4).

Who, when He was reviled, reviled not again;

when He suffered, He threatened not; but committed Himself to Him that **judges** righteously (1 Peter 2:23).

JUDGMENT (DECREE)

Therefore the ungodly shall not stand in the **judgment**, nor sinners in the congregation of the righteous (Psalms 1:5).

Arise, O LORD, in your anger, lift up thyself because of the rage of mine enemies: and awake for me to the **judgment** that thou hast commanded (Psalms 7:6).

The **judgments** of the LORD are true and righteous altogether (Psalms 19:9).

Thy righteousness is like the great mountains; thy **judgments** are a great deep: O LORD, thou preserves man and beast (Psalms 36:6).

For the LORD loves **judgment**, and forsakes not his saints (Psalms 37:28).

The mouth of the righteous speaks wisdom, and his tongue talks of **judgment** (Psalms 37:30).

Thou didst cause judgment to be heard from heaven; the earth feared, and was still, When God arose to **judgment**, to save all the meek of the earth (Psalms 76:8-9).

But **judgment** shall return unto righteousness: and all the upright in heart shall follow it (Psalms 94:15).

You establish equity, you execute **judgment** and righteousness (Psalms 99:4).

The LORD executes righteousness and **judgment** for all that are oppressed (Psalms 103:6).

The works of His hands are verity and **judgment**; all his commandments are sure (Psalms 111:7).

Teach me good **judgment** and knowledge: for I have believed thy commandments (Psalms 119:66).

Let the high praises of God be in their mouth, and a two-edged sword in their hand; To execute vengeance upon the heathen, and punishments upon the people; To bind their kings with chains, and their nobles with fetters of iron; To execute upon them the written **judgment** (Psalms 149:6-8).

JUDGMENTS

Then shall I not be ashamed, when I have respect unto all thy commandments. I will praise thee with uprightness of heart, when I shall have learned thy righteous **judgments** (Psalms 119:6, 7).

With my lips have I declared all the **judgments** of thy mouth (Psalms 119:13).

If his children forsake my law, and walk not in my **judgments**; 1 If they break my statutes, and keep not my commandments; Then will I visit their transgression with the rod, and their iniquity with stripes" (Psalms 89:30-32).

Remember His marvelous works that He has done; His wonders, and the **judgments** of His mouth; O ye seed of Abraham his servant, ye children of Jacob His chosen. He is the LORD our God: His **judgments** are in all the earth (Psalms 105:5-7).

Remove from me the way of lying: and grant me thy law graciously. I have chosen the way of truth: thy **judgments** have I laid before me (Psalms 119:29-30).

I remembered thy **judgments** of old, O LORD; and have comforted myself (Psalms 119:52).

At midnight I will rise to give thanks unto thee because of thy righteous **judgments** (Psalms 119:62).

I know, O LORD, that thy **judgments** are right, and that thou in faithfulness hast afflicted me (Psalms 119:75).

I have sworn, and I will perform it, that I will

keep thy righteous **judgments** (Psalms 119:106).

Whosoever is angry with his brother without a cause shall be in danger of the **judgment**: and whosoever shall say to his brother, Raca, shall be in danger of the council: but whosoever shall say, Thou fool, shall be in danger of hell fire (Matthew 5:22).

Who knowing the **judgment** of God, that they which commit such things are worthy of death, not only do the same, but have pleasure in them that do them (Roman 1:32).

For the **judgment** was by one to condemnation, but the free gift is of many offences unto justification (Romans 5:16).

Therefore as by the offence of one **judgment** came upon all men to condemnation; even so by the righteousness of one the free gift came upon all men unto justification of life (Roman 5:18).

And the angels which kept not their first estate, but left their own habitation, he hath reserved in everlasting chains under darkness unto the **judgment** of the great day (Jude 1:6).

JUSTICE

He shall judge the world in righteousness, He shall minister **justice** to the people in uprightness (Psalms 9:8).

Justice and judgment are the habitation of thy throne: mercy and truth shall go before thy face (Psalm 89:14).

Blessed are they that keep **justice**, and he that doeth righteousness at all times (Psalms 106:3).

I have done judgment and **justice**: leave me not to mine oppressors (Psalms 119:121).

Who executes **justice** for the oppressed: who gives food to the hungry. The LORD gives freedom the prisoners (Psalms 146:7).

I will make **justice** a measuring line, and righteousness a plummet (Isaiah 28:17).

For the LORD is a God of **justice**: blessed are all they that wait for him (Isaiah 30:18).

Behold my servant, whom I uphold; mine elect, in whom my soul delights; I have put my spirit upon him: he shall bring forth **justice** to the Gentiles (Isaiah 42:1).

He shall not fail nor be discouraged, till He has set **justice** in the earth: and the isles shall wait for His law (Isaiah 42:4).

I the LORD loves **justice** (Isaiah 66:1).

Now I Nebuchadnezzar praise and extol and honor the King of heaven, all whose works are truth, and His ways **justice**: and those that walk in pride he is able to abase (Daniel 4:37).

Thus says the LORD of hosts, saying, Execute true **justice**, and show mercy and compassions every man to his brother (Zechariah 7:9).

Peace be with you!

If this book was helpful to you, I would love to hear from you. Please send your comments/ Questions to the author by email: lydiaeelyon@gmail.com
Or Text +268 76616611

Be blessed!!!

Apostle Lydia E'Elyon

All rights reserved© 2021

www.ingramcontent.com/pod-product-compliance
Lightning Source LLC
Chambersburg PA
CBHW020636220526
45464CB00001B/168